The FABRIC and NEEDLECRAFT PROJECT BOOK

The FABRIC and NEEDLECRAFT PROJECT BOOK

Sebastian Kelly

HOW TO USE THE MEASUREMENTS

All craftspeople have their own way of working and feel most comfortable calculating in their preferred measurements. So, where applicable, the option of metric, imperial and cup measures are given. The golden rule is to choose only one set of measurements and to stick with it throughout each project to ensure accurate results.

PUBLISHER'S NOTE

Crafts and hobbies are great fun to learn and can fill many hours of rewarding leisure time, but some general points should be remembered for safety and care of the environment.

☛ *Always choose non-toxic materials wherever possible, for example paints, glue and varnishes. Where these are not suitable, use materials in a well-ventilated area and always follow the manufacturer's instructions.*

☛ *Craft knives, needles, scissors sewing machines and all sharp implements should be used with care. Always use a cutting board or mat to avoid damage to household surfaces (it is also safer to cut onto a firm, hard surface).*

☛ *Protect surfaces from paint, glue and varnish splashes by laying down old newspapers, plastic sheeting or an old sheet.*

SOME USEFUL TERMS

US	UK
Clear rubbing alcohol	*White spirit*
Flat latex	*Matt emulsion paint*
Grease pencil	*Chinagraph pencil*
Heavy-weight iron-on fabric	*Heavy pelmet vilene*
Posterboard	*Card*
Styrofoam	*Polystyrene*
Upholstery fabric	*Furnishing fabric*
White glue	*PVA glue*
Zipper	*Zip*

This edition published in 1997 by
Sebastian Kelly
2 Rectory Road
Oxford OX4 1BW

© Anness Publishing Limited 1994

Produced by Anness Publishing Limited

ISBN 1 901688 21 6

Publisher: Joanna Lorenz
Project Editor: Penelope Cream
Editorial Assistant: Charles Moxham
Designer: Hall Design
Photographer: Martin Norris
Illustrators: Vana Haggerty and John Hutchinson

Printed in Singapore by Star Standard Industries Pte. Ltd.

1 3 5 7 9 10 8 6 4 2

CONTENTS

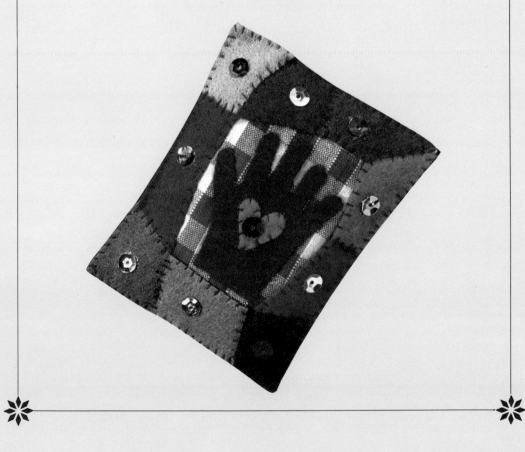

TINY TRINKET BOX

A little triangular tartan box, lined with silk, would make a delightful gift either on its own or containing a tiny surprise.

YOU WILL NEED
Tracing paper
Pencil
Template plastic
50 cm (½ yd) fusible woven heavy-weight iron-on interlining
Scissors
25 cm (10 in) square of tartan fabric
25 cm (10 in) square of silk fabric for lining
50 cm (½ yd) square of brushed cotton for interlining
Steam iron
Needle and thread

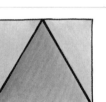

1 Size up and trace the triangular and oblong shapes onto template plastic. Using a sharp pencil, draw four triangles and six oblongs on the iron-on interlining. Cut them out, then slightly trim two of the triangles and three of the oblongs for the lining.

2 Cut out two triangles and three oblongs from the tartan and lining silk leaving a 6 mm (¼ in) seam allowance all round. Cut double the amount from the brushed cotton but without seam allowances.

3 Place the tartan pieces wrong side up on an ironing board. Cover them with the brushed cotton pieces, then the iron-on interlining, sticky side up. Press the fabric seam allowance up onto the sticky side with the tip of the iron. Leave to cool. Repeat with the silk lining pieces.

4 Press the tartan fronts and silk linings together, wrong sides facing, until they fuse. Leave to cool. Whip stitch the pieces in place.

5 Whip stitch the three sides of the box to the base, right sides together. Pull up the sides of the box and slip stitch together. Slip stitch along the hinge of the lid.

NAPKIN RINGS AND NAPKINS

Matching napkin rings and napkins give a table a festive look for a special lunch or dinner party. These are quick to make using tartan ribbons and pelmet interlining.

YOU WILL NEED
25 cm (¼ yd) fusible woven heavy-
   weight iron-on interlining
Scissors
2 m × 12 mm (2 yd × ½ in) tartan
   ribbon
Iron
Stapler
Needle and thread
1 m × 115 cm (1 yd × 45 in) red
   fabric

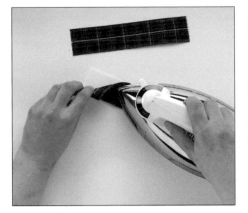

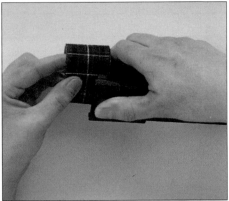

1 For each napkin ring, cut out a piece of iron-on interlining 15 cm × 4 cm (6 in × 1½ in) and a matching length of tartan ribbon. Iron the ribbon onto the sticky side of the pelmet interlining. Leave to cool.

2 Bend into a circle and secure with two staples.

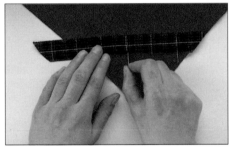

3 Make a looped decoration with the tartan ribbon and sew in place over the join. Cut the ends of the ribbon diagonally.

4 Cut out four napkins 45 cm (18 in) square in the red fabric. Sew a strip of tartan ribbon diagonally across one corner of each napkin.

5 Trim all the corners diagonally to reduce bulk. Turn in a small hem and sew. Press well.

EVENING TOTE-BAG

Jewel-coloured velvet is the ideal fabric for this capacious evening tote-bag. Twisted gold knitting yarn forms the cord.

YOU WILL NEED
Tracing paper
Pencil
Stencil card
Craft knife
Double-sided tape
Scissors
50 cm × 152 cm (½ yd × 60 in) velvet
Paper
Masking tape
Gold spray paint
Gold knitting yarn for the cord
50 cm × 115 cm (½ yd × 45 in) gold lining
Pins
Needle and thread
Safety pin or bodkin
Gilt bead

1 Scale up and trace the fleur-de-lys template. Scribble on the back of the paper with a soft pencil to make a carbon. Turn over and draw over the lines of the motif onto stencil card. Cut out the motif with a craft knife. Stick small pieces of double-sided sticky tape on the back to hold the stencil onto the fabric.

2 Cut out two pieces of velvet 55 cm × 38 cm (21½ in × 15 in). Centre the stencil motif on the fabric and press gently so that the sticky tape holds. Place paper over the remaining fabric to prevent the paint from spreading and hold in place with masking tape. Shake the can of spray paint according to the manufacturer's instructions. Spray and leave to dry thoroughly before removing the stencil.

3 Meanwhile, make a twisted cord. Measure out 8 strands of yarn, each 4.5 m (15 ft) long, which will give you a finished length of about 2 m (6 ft 6 in). Hook the strands of yarn at one end over a window catch or door handle, and tie a knot in the other end. Slip a pencil through the end and twist tightly until the yarn forms a cord. Tie a knot at the other end, then tie another two knots about 10 cm (4 in) from one end. Cut between these two knots, and use this 10 cm (4 in) length to make a loop.

4 Cut out two pieces of lining 55 cm × 38 cm (21½ in × 15 in). Pin the linings to the tops of each of the velvet pieces.

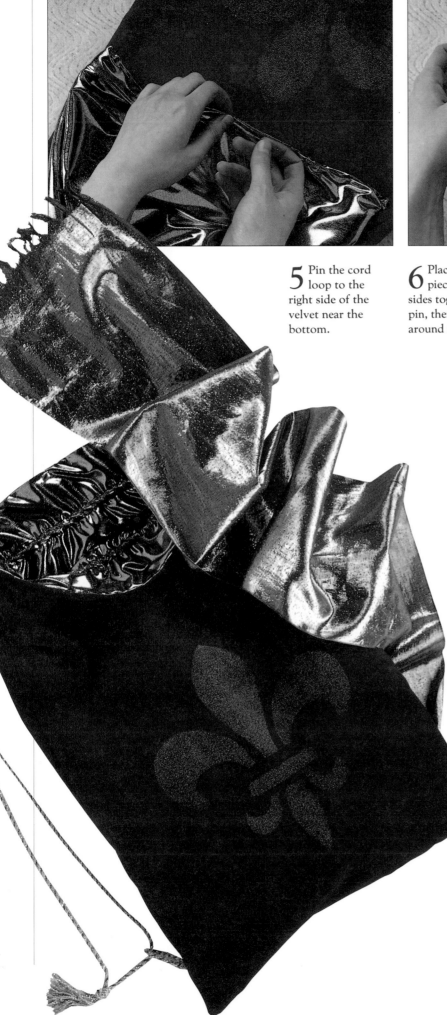

5 Pin the cord loop to the right side of the velvet near the bottom.

6 Place the two pieces right sides together and pin, then tack, around three sides, leaving a gap open at the bottom of the linings. This will enable you to turn it through. Turn through to the right side and make a double seam along the bottom of the lining to close.

7 Tuck the lining into the bag and tack along the top edge, and again 5 cm (2 in) further down. Machine two lines next to this tacking line, about 2.5 cm (1 in) apart to form a channel. Open a few stitches in one seam so that the cord can pass through the channel. Thread through, using a bodkin or a safety pin.

8 Pass both ends of the cord through a gilt bead, then through the loop. Tie the ends together and cut to form a tassel.

DUCK PINCUSHION

A firm and colourful duck to keep all your pins out of trouble, easily made from oddments of material and decorated in different ways. Silk or felt are particularly effective fabrics to work with.

YOU WILL NEED
Metal rule
Plain paper
Pencil
Scissors
Pins
Piece of left-over fabric, about 38 cm × 28 cm (15 in × 11 in)
Needle and thread
Polyester stuffing (batting)
2 small glass beads
30 cm × 12 mm (12 in × ½ in) ribbon

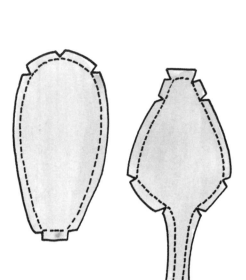

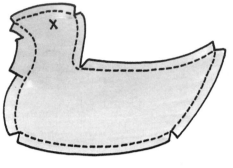

1 Scale up the template, transfer onto paper and cut out. Pin the patterns onto the fabric and cut out, leaving 6 mm (¼ in) all round each piece for the seam allowances.

2 Pin the four pieces together and stitch along the joins, leaving the front of neck open where marked. Turn the duck inside out and push the stuffing (batting) through the neck hole until the duck is firm. Sew on the glass beads for the eyes. Sew up the neck hole and cover the join with a piece of ribbon. Pleat remaining ribbon and add to the tail.

BOLSTER
CUSHION

Brighten up your living room with
an elegant bolster cushion, using a
patterned furnishing fabric that
reflects your colour scheme.

YOU WILL NEED

Tape measure
Bolster cushion, about 45 cm (18 in)
  long
Furnishing fabric to fit cushion
Scissors
Iron
Zip about 41 cm (16 in)
Pins
Needle and thread
Thin card
Wadding (batting) for end circles
30 cm (12 in) square of silk for end
  circles
Fray check liquid

1 Measure the length and circumference of the cushion.

2 Cut out the fabric to these measurements adding seam allowances. Press in these allowances, one 12 mm (½ in) and one 15 mm (⅝ in), on two opposite long sides. Mark the centre of sides and of the zip. Pin, tack (baste) and sew in place using a zipper foot if sewing by machine. The side with the smaller seam allowance should be sewn with the zip closed and the other side with the zip open.

3 Turn the cover through and insert the cushion, centrally. Pleat into folds and pin the two ends. Take out the cushion and sew the pleats in place.

4 Cut out two circles of card about 5 cm (2 in) in diameter and two circles of wadding (batting) the same size. Cut out two of silk 10 cm (4 in) in diameter. Apply fray check and run a tacking (basting) stitch just inside one silk circle.

5 Place over a card circle and wadding (batting), pulling up the thread to tighten and finishing with a knot. Repeat with the other silk circle. Insert the bolster cushion into the cover. Pin a covered circle in the centre of each end and stitch in place.

VELVET PURSE

Unusual evening bags, just large enough for lipstick, comb and purse are hard to find. Here velvet and silk are combined to give the finishing touch to a party outfit.

YOU WILL NEED
Tracing paper
Pencil
Scissors
Pins
30 cm × 115 cm (⅓ yd × 45 in) velvet
30 cm × 115 cm (⅓ yd × 45 in) silk
Needle and thread
Lurex knitting yarn
Safety pin or bodkin
Pearl beads

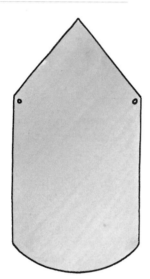

1 Using the template for guidance, transfer the pattern onto tracing paper to measure 43 cm (17 in) from base to tip by 25 cm (10 in) wide. Place on the velvet and cut out two pieces, making sure that the pile of the fabric lies the same way on both pieces. Cut out two lining pieces from the silk. Pin and tack (baste) the 'points' right sides together. Machine sew and trim the tip. Turn through and tack (baste) along the edges.

2 Keeping the 'points' out of the way, join the fronts of the velvet and the silk lining together. Machine sew, leaving the base of the lining open for turning.

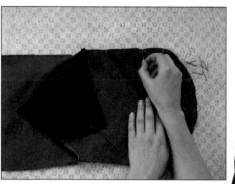

3 Before turning, snip 'V' shapes out of the seam allowance around the curves, taking care not to snip the stitching.

4 Turn the bag through, by putting your hand inside, grasping the base and pulling. Close the lining with a seam and tuck it into the bag.

5 Smooth the bag so that the two fabrics lie flat, then pin and run two lines of tacking (basting) as shown on the pattern. Sew along these lines which will form the channel for the cord.

6 Make the twisted cord by knotting eight strands of lurex knitting yarn about 90 cm (36 in) long to a hook or drawer knob. Stretch the yarn out and knot the ends together, then trim. Place a pencil in the loop and twist in one direction until the yarn is sufficiently tightly twisted to curl into a firm cord. Mark the centre, then knot the other ends. These cords are easier to make with two people twisting in opposite directions!

7 Undo a couple of stitches along one side of the seam and using a safety pin or bodkin thread the cord through.

8 Knot both ends together, then cut to make a tassel. If you would prefer a shoulder strap, make the cord longer. Decorate with pearls sewn along the edges of the 'points'. Remove the tacking (basting) threads.

DIARY COVER

Diaries often have dull covers, so here is a way to personalize them using brightly coloured checked silk.

YOU WILL NEED
Diary
Plain paper
Pencil
Ruler
Scissors
30 cm × 115 cm (⅓ yd × 45 in) silk
Fray check liquid
Double-sided tape
2 pieces of wadding (batting) to fit
Pins
Needle and thread

1 Measure the diary by placing it on a large piece of paper and drawing around the open front, spine and back. Add a fold allowance of 4 cm (1½ in). Cut out the paper and place it on the silk. Using a soft pencil, draw the shape.

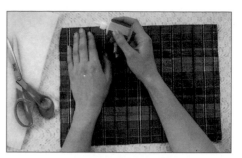

2 Cut out the silk and use a fray check liquid along the edges to prevent the silk fraying.

3 Put a couple of pieces of double-sided tape on each side of the diary cover.

4 Remove the backing paper from the tape and wrap the wadding (batting) around the diary, pressing onto the tape.

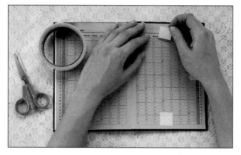

5 Place some pieces of double-sided tape around the edges of the inside cover, peel off the backing paper and wrap the silk around, making sure you have an equal amount of fabric on each side to fold in.

6 Make a diagonal cut on each side of the spine and fold the corners diagonally by tucking the spare fabric under.

7 Fold the corners of the silk in and fold the edges over diagonally. Pin in place. Hold in place with a slip stitch, trimming the spine a little further if necessary.

FABRIC LAMPSHADE

Trim a lampshade frame to match your living room in contrasting or co-ordinating fabric. Short lengths of left-over material are very useful for this type of project, and you can choose the size of wire frame according to the amount of fabric available. Be sure not to use a fabric that has a very low resistance to heat, such as some man-made fibres.

YOU WILL NEED

Wire lampshade frame
Tape measure
Length of fabric to cover frame with a
    seam allowance of 5 cm (2 in)
Same amount of pale lining fabric
Scissors
Pins
Needle and thread
Safety pin
Length of elastic equal to length of
    fabric
Braid to trim

1 To determine the amount of fabric needed, measure the height of the wire frame and its circum- ference. Add 5 cm (2 in) for the seam allowance. Cut the lining fabric to the same dimensions.

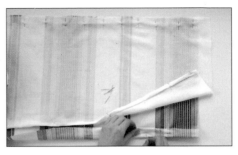

2 Turn over the top and bottom seam allowances on both pieces and pin. Sew the edges of the two pieces of fabric together on the top only; sew two lines of stitches, leaving a channel for the elastic.

3 Attach a safety pin to one end of the elastic and thread it through the channel, keeping hold of the other end. Holding the two ends together, place the main fabric over the shade, pull the elastic tight so that the shade sits well on the frame and sew the ends of the elastic together. Stitch up the seam in the fabric.

4 Grasp the lining and pull it down, stretching the main fabric taut over the frame.

5 Tuck the lining down inside the shade, and pin and sew in place at the top. Trim the edges with braid.

Working by hand

Although some appliqué designs are worked with machine satin stitch, you can work the stitching by hand if you prefer. Follow the project instructions in the usual way, but substitute buttonhole stitch for machine satin stitch. Work the stitch in a suitable embroidery thread such as stranded cotton.

Working machine appliqué

Always work a small practice piece before starting to machine stitch or machine appliqué in order to check that your thread, needle, stitch size and fabric are compatible. Fit a new needle before starting to sew as a blunt one will damage the fabric and result in uneven stitching.

To work satin stitch, set your machine to a zigzag stitch about 3 mm (⅛ in) wide and 6 mm (¼ in) long. Use a special appliqué foot if one is provided with your machine. Test the stitch on a spare piece of fabric, practising points and corners, and adjust your machine as necessary. A piece of typing paper placed beneath your fabric on top of the sewing machine plate will help when puckering is a problem – stitch the design then tear away the paper round the stitches.

Start stitching at the beginning of a straight edge and do not go too fast. When working intricate shapes, go carefully and turn the wheel by hand to make one stitch at a time. Pivot at the corner of shapes by leaving the needle in the fabric, raising the presser foot and turning the fabric before lowering the foot and continuing to stitch. Never turn the wheel of the machine backwards as this will damage the machine.

Using fusible bonding paper

Cut out a piece of fusible, iron-on bonding paper slightly larger than the shape to be applied. Cover the wrong side of the shape with the paper, placing it adhesive side down. Press

in place, setting the iron to the correct temperature for the fabric. Allow to cool, then cut out the shape. Peel off the backing paper and place the shape with the adhesive side down onto the right side of the background fabric. Carefully press the shape in place using either a steam iron or a dry iron and a damp cloth. Make sure you allow the fabric to dry thoroughly before you begin to stitch.

Blanket stitch

Use blanket stitch for appliqué when working with a fabric such as felt which does not fray. When applying other types of fabric by hand, choose buttonhole stitch instead.

Work blanket stitch from left to right, pulling the needle through the fabric over the top of the working thread. Space the stitches evenly along the row.

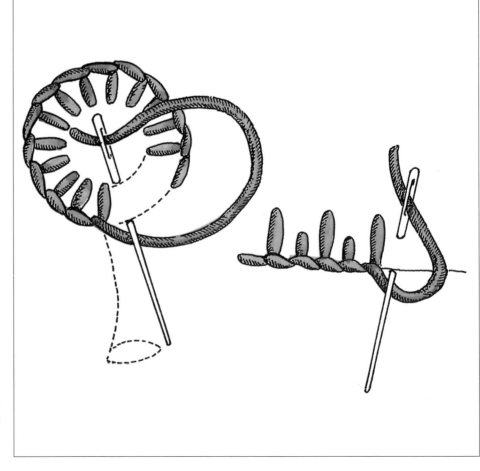

Satin stitch

Use satin stitch to fill small shapes with stitching.

Take large stitches across the surface of the fabric, as shown, then return the thread underneath the fabric and bring the needle out close to the previous stitch. Work the stitches close together so the fabric is adequately covered.

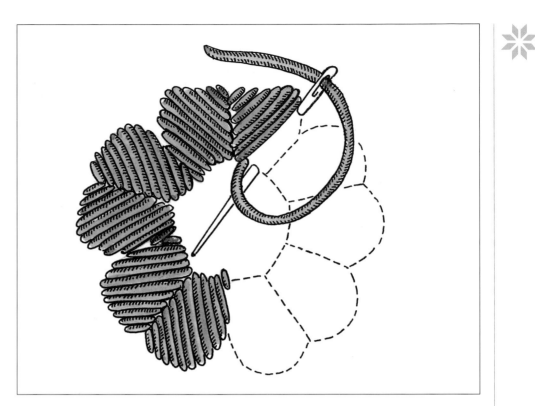

Running stitch

This is the most basic embroidery stitch and you can achieve varying effects by altering the spacing between the stitches.

Work running stitch by passing the needle smoothly in and out of the fabric.

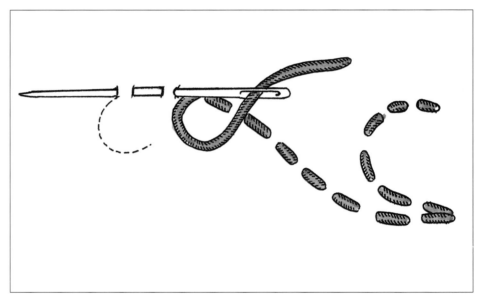

Buttonhole stitch

Use buttonhole stitch as an edging stitch for appliqué.

Work buttonhole stitch from left to right in the same way as blanket stitch, pulling the needle through the fabric over the top of the working thread. Work the stitches close together so that no fabric is visible between them.

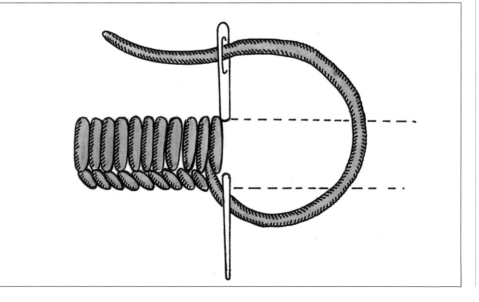

PATCH POCKET

This heart-shaped pocket in red felt looks very striking on a dark dress. Be sure to use a washable felt unless the dress has to be dry-cleaned.

YOU WILL NEED
Red felt
Scissors
Tracing paper
Pencil
Needle
Green and white embroidery thread

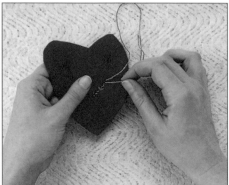

1 Cut out two heart shapes from the red felt and one in tracing paper. Draw a flower on the paper heart and trace the design onto one of the felt hearts.

2 Stitch the stem using green embroidery thread.

3 Stitch the flowers using white embroidery thread.

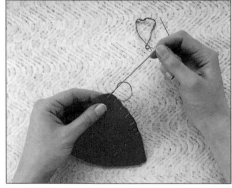

4 Using blanket stitch and green embroidery thread, sew the two hearts together to form a pocket and then sew into place on the dress.

APPLIQUÉD T-SHIRT

A plain white T-shirt can be quickly brightened up and made stylish enough for a gift, using appliquéd felt and jazzy beads. For a more ornate look, reduce the spacing between the beads or add longer stripes in the same pattern.

YOU WILL NEED
Tape measure
White T-shirt
Pins
Needle and tacking (basting) thread
Remnants of brightly coloured felt
Scissors
Embroidery thread
Beads and sequins
Steam iron

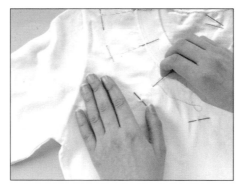

1 Measure the neck opening of the T-shirt and mark the centre front with a pin. From this point, measure and pin every 5 cm (2 in) around the front of the neck opening. From each pin, measure down 5 cm (2 in) and mark with another pin. Tack (baste) between the pins with small stitches. Remove the pins.

2 Cut out 14 felt circles, about 20 mm (¾ in) in diameter. Pin one at each end of the tacking (basting) stitches and another about 12 mm (½ in) along. Blanket stitch each circle of felt in position, using a contrasting colour of embroidery thread. Sew the beads and sequins between the circles. Remove the tacking (basting) and press.

CHARACTER CUSHION

This cushion with a stylized appliquéd animal head is ideal for a child's room. Fine features are worked in a satin stitch. Remember to choose fabrics of similar weights and make sure they are all machine washable.

YOU WILL NEED
Ruler
Tracing paper
Pencil
Scissors
Pins
30 cm (12 in) square beige fabric for head
Remnants of green, pink, white and black fabric
50 cm × 1 m (½ yd × 39 in) blue fabric for features
Needle and thread
36 cm (14 in) cushion pad

1 Scale up the template to the required size. Trace over each separate section of the design, label for colour and cut out the shape. Pin each piece of tracing paper onto the correct colour fabric and cut out.

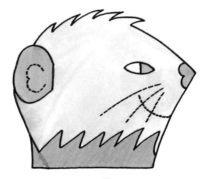

2 Cut out a 36 cm (14 in) square of the blue fabric for the front of the cushion, including 3 cm (1¼ in) seam allowance. Pin the different coloured pieces onto this square, adjusting if necessary.

3 Sew each piece into place using a running stitch. Go over the running stitches with a satin, close-set zigzag stitch. When all the material is sewn into place, sew on the other features such as whiskers and remove the pins.

4 To complete the cushion, cut the remaining blue fabric into two pieces, each measuring 36 cm × 24 cm (14 in × 9½ in) to allow for overlaps. Sew the pieces of fabric onto the back of the appliquéd panel so that the edges overlap forming an envelope. Insert the cushion pad.

BROIDERY PERSE APRON

The appliqué roses on this apron will bring summer memories to the kitchen all the year round. The roses shown here were taken from a sample of furnishing fabric; they were applied using fusible bonding paper and satin stitched on the machine.

YOU WILL NEED

1 m × 115 cm (1 yd × 45 in) striped
    fabric
Scissors
Fusible iron-on bonding paper
Piece of printed fabric with some large
    flowers
Steam iron
Tape measure
1.5 m (60 in) tape or ribbon for ties
Pins

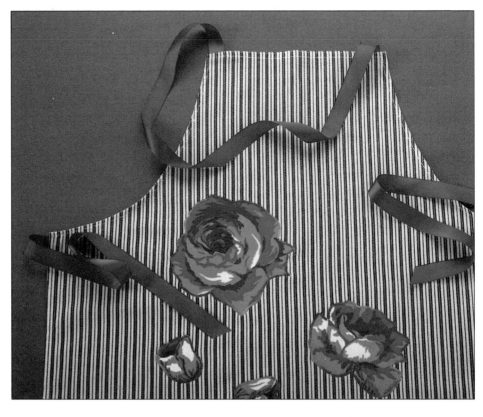

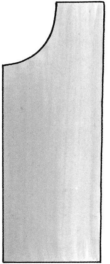

Fabric folded double

1 Scale up the template and transfer to striped fabric. Cut out. Cut out large enough pieces of fusible bonding paper to cover the chosen flowers and apply to the wrong side of the printed fabric using a steam iron. Measure the length of tape or ribbon required for the head loop and cut. Divide the remaining ribbon in half for the waist ties and cut the ends diagonally.

2 Trim around the edge of the flowers.

3 Peel off the backing paper, then iron the flowers onto the front of the apron. Machine satin stitch around the flowers. It will help to keep the stitches flat if you place a piece of paper between the plate of the sewing machine and the back of the fabric. This may be torn away afterwards.

4 Pin the waist ties and head loop in position, then turn in a small hem and machine stitch all the way round the apron. Reinforce the head loop with an extra row of machine stitches.

APPLIQUÉD POT HOLDER

The technique used for making this decorative pot holder is known as Hawaiian appliqué. By using felt for the motif, there is no need to hem it which saves time. Remember to buy washable felt as pot holders need washing frequently!

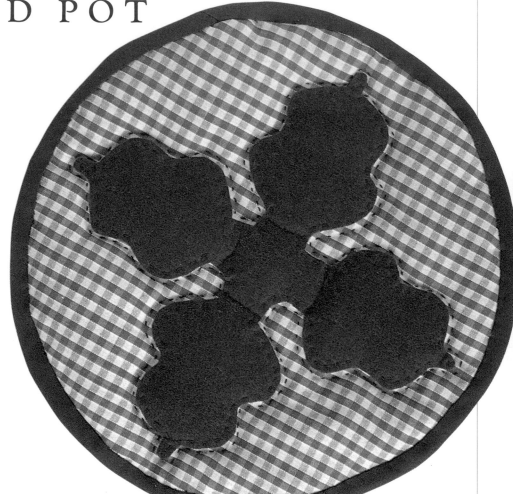

YOU WILL NEED
Tracing paper
Pencil
Pins
20 cm (8 in) square of washable felt
Scissors
Plain paper
25 cm × 115 cm (¼ yd × 45 in) gingham
Square of double-thickness wadding (batting)
Needle and thread
Iron
Bias binding

1 Design a motif and trace it. Pin it onto the felt and cut it out. Cut out a circle in plain paper and place on the gingham. Using the paper template as a guide cut out two gingham circles.

2 Centre the felt motif on one gingham circle and pin, then tack in place. Appliqué, with a small running stitch, just inside the motif. Press gently when finished.

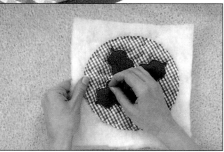

3 Place the back, wadding (batting) and top together, then pin. Quilt with a small running stitch, just outside the motif.

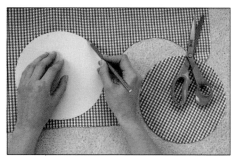

4 Pin firmly, then tack around the edge of the circle. Trim away the excess wadding (batting).

5 Measure the circumference of the pot holder and cut a slightly longer strip of bias binding. Make a loop with more bias binding and pin to the pot holder.

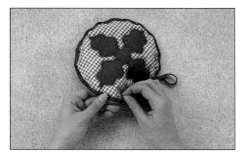

6 Join the two ends of the bias binding strip with a diagonal seam, and fold the bias binding around the pot holder. Pin, tack and sew either by machine or by hand.

TABLE RUNNER

This runner will decorate and protect the centre of any dining-room table while not in use. All the motifs are slightly different so you can cut out by eye and arrange the pieces as you go along. If you want to plan to size, cut out a piece of paper to the same dimensions as the table top and lay pieces of tracing paper cut to shape on top.

YOU WILL NEED
Felt in an assortment of colours
Scissors
Contrasting embroidery thread
Needle
Small pearl buttons

2 Sew around the edges of the small heart in blanket stitch.

1 Cut out enough large and small felt hearts in contrasting colours to fill the outer diamonds of the pattern. Place a small heart in the centre of a large heart and join in the centre with a few stitches of embroidery thread.

3 Cut a rectangle of felt to fit the size of the table. Cut out the diamonds that will go around the outer edge of the runner. Place the pair of hearts in the centre of the diamond and sew on using blanket stitch. Make up the floral motifs for the inner diamonds in the same way using coloured felt and blanket stitch.

4 Position all the diamonds on the felt background. Attach the diamonds by the corners, stitching one small pearl button at the same time onto each corner. Add extra buttons for decoration on the floral motifs.

HEART MOBILE

This pretty heart mobile glistens and sparkles as it moves, catching the light on the beads and jewels. Use contrasting colours of felt and vary the sizes of the hearts to create an eye-catching effect.

YOU WILL NEED

Plain paper
Pencil
Pinking shears
Pins
25 cm (10 in) squares of felt in bright colours
50 cm (½ yd) of 60 g (2 oz) wadding (batting), optional
Needle and embroidery thread
Scissors
Assortment of imitation jewels, beads and sequins
Coat hanger

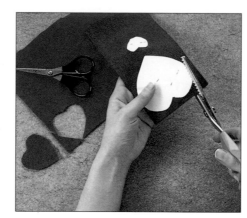

1 Draw heart shapes of different sizes on paper and cut out the patterns using pinking shears. Pin the patterns onto the felt squares, and cut out a front and a back for each large heart shape. Cut out a medium-sized heart shape for each large heart, and a piece of wadding (batting), if stuffing the hearts.

2 Decorate each tiny heart with imitation jewels, pressing the studs over each jewel to hold it in place. Sew on using brightly coloured thread and running stitch.

3 Sew a tiny heart onto each medium-sized heart.

4 Sew each medium-sized heart onto a large heart. Decorate both the front and the back of each motif.

5 Sew each front and back together using a running stitch as close to the edge as possible, leaving a small gap to insert the wadding (batting) if using. Tie the hearts onto a coat hanger that can then be moved from place to place to catch the draught.

VALENTINE BROOCH AND EARRINGS

Tell someone you love them by making these hand-stitched valentine earrings and brooch. You could use fabric for the appliqué, although felt is much easier to use as it does not fray.

YOU WILL NEED
Tracing paper
Black felt-tip pen
Scissors
Oddments of brightly coloured felt
Needle and thread
2 short headpins
Fabric glue
Sequins
2 kidney wires or ear-clips
Oddment of cotton fabric
Pins
Stuffing (batting)
3cm (1¼ in) straight brooch clip

1 For the earrings, scale up the hand and heart templates, transfer to the felt and cut out two hands and one heart. Using very small stitches, sew the heart in the centre of the hand.

2 Sew one side of the hands together. Position a headpin in the middle so that the end protrudes. Glue in place. Sew the edges of the hand and figures together. Glue sequins onto the fingertips and one in the centre of the hand. Hang the earrings on a kidney wire or ear-clip. Repeat for the other earring, making sure that the hand and heart face in the opposite direction.

3 For the brooch, cut out the small rectangular paper base template. Cut out one piece of fabric, and one of felt for the brooch back. Trace the geometric templates numbered 1–9 and cut out of fabric, leaving a small seam allowance around each shape. Pin them in place on the fabric front and, using very small stitches, sew them down.

4 Trace the hand and heart templates and cut out of felt. Using very small stitches, sew them onto the centre of the brooch front.

5 Pin and sew the back to the front, leaving the bottom seam open. Stuff, then sew. Sew the clip onto the back 20 mm (¾ in) down from brooch top. Glue on the sequins.

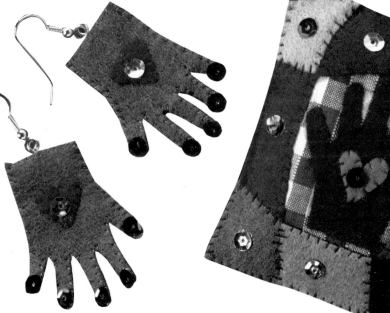

QUILTING TECHNIQUES

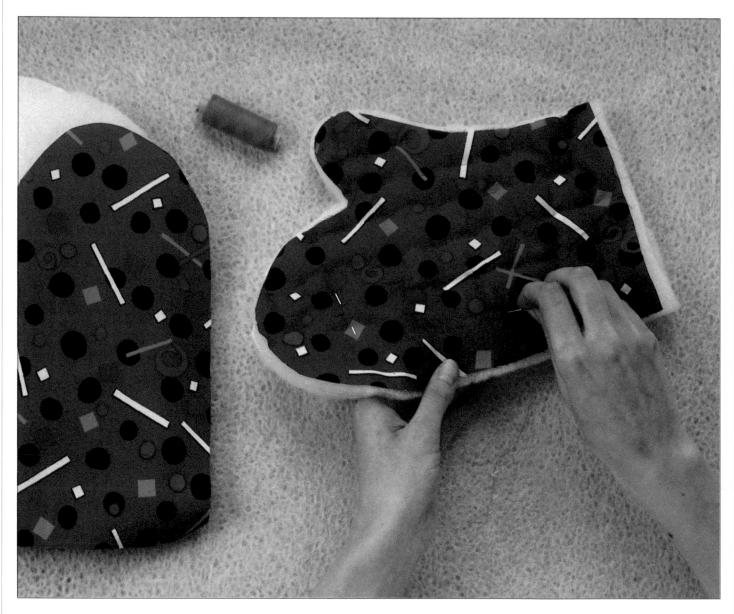

Tacking for quilting

To achieve good results, the layers of fabric you are working with when quilting – usually top fabric, wadding (batting) and backing fabric – need to be secured together before you begin to stitch. This will prevent the layers from slipping and sliding out of position. To do this, lay the backing fabric wrong side up on a flat, hard surface such as a table and secure it with strips of masking tape at the corners. Lay the other two layers over the top, ending with the top fabric, right side up, and secure them with tape in the same way. Carefully pin the layers together,

working from the centre outwards, remove the masking tape, then work lines of tacking (basting) stitches about 10 cm (4 in) apart both across and down the piece. Begin each row of tacking at the centre using a long length of thread and leave half of it hanging in the middle so you can re-thread your needle to complete the row in the other direction. Remove all the tacking stitches when your quilted design is complete.

For small pieces of quilting, you can use safety pins instead of tacking stitches, but make sure that the pins will not leave visible holes in the fabric when they are removed.

Quilting by hand

Work the quilting design using small, evenly spaced running stitches. Thread your needle with about 45 cm (18 in) of thread and make a small knot at the long end. Insert the needle into the top fabric a little distance away from the line to be quilted and gently tug the knot through to hide it beneath the fabric.

To finish the thread, make two or three tiny stitches where the row of running stitches ends, then take the needle through the filling and pull the thread through the top fabric a short distance away. Cut off the thread end flush with the surface.

Applying bias binding

Pin the bias binding on the right side of the fabric with right sides facing and raw edges aligning. Tack (baste) and machine stitch in position with a 6 mm (¼ in) seam allowance. Remove the tacking stitches, turn the free edge of the binding over to the wrong side of the fabric and slip stitch with matching thread to secure in place.

Quilting by machine

Work a small practice piece before starting to machine quilt to check that your thread, needle, stitch size and fabric are compatible and if necessary adjust these until you achieve the desired result. A 'walking foot' fitted to your machine will help prevent the fabric layers moving and causing puckering. A stitch length of about 8 stitches to 2.5 cm (1 in) works well for quilting, but you may need to alter this to suit the particular fabric you are using. Take time to fit a new needle each time you begin making a project as a blunt one will damage the fabric and cause uneven stitching.

Slip stitch

Use slip stitch for joining two folded fabric edges together or when securing bias binding. When joining two folds, the stitches are almost invisible and are worked from the right side.

Place the two folded edges together with right sides facing you, slip the needle along inside the fold of one edge, take the needle across to the other edge and slip it along that fold. Pull the thread to draw the edges together.

Running stitch

Use running stitch for hand quilting designs, keeping the stitches small and evenly spaced on both the front and back of the piece.

Work running stitch by passing the needle regularly in and out of the fabric to create the pattern.

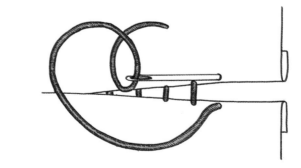

COT TOY BAG

Early-rising tots will be delighted to find this toy bag hanging at the end of the cot. It is easily made from a furnishing fabric in a design that would appeal to a small child. Here the animal squares have been cut out from a much larger overall pattern, joined and quilted. Measure the width and height of the cot to obtain the bag dimensions.

YOU WILL NEED

Furnishing fabric with some eye-catching motifs
Scissors
Flat wadding (batting)
Fabric for bag back
Backing muslin (calico)
Lining fabric
Pins
Needle and thread
Iron

1 Cut out patterns from the furnishing fabric, allowing 6 mm (¼ in) for seams. Cut out one piece of flat wadding (batting), one piece of fabric for the back, one piece of muslin and two pieces of lining to the required size.

2 Pin, tack and sew the patterned squares together. Press the seams open flat.

3 Lay the muslin on a flat surface, cover with the wadding (batting) and then the patterned squares, right side up. Pin, then tack the three layers together.

4 Machine or hand quilt around the animals, neatly knotting the ends of the threads to finish off.

5 Pin and sew on the backing fabric. Cut loops and binding from the backing fabric 4 cm (1½ in) wide to fit around the top of the bag and make two loops to fit the cot. Fold the loops lengthways and zigzag stitch to neaten the edges. Machine sew the three sides of the bag lining. Join the back and front of the bag, right sides together, and turn through. Drop the lining into the bag and shake down into place. Pin the loops in place and pin the binding around the top of the bag. Sew, then turn the binding to the inside and slip stitch.

OVEN GLOVE

An oven glove made from a lively fabric is sure to bring a smile to any cook's face. Matching sets of gloves can be made to co-ordinate with the kitchen colour scheme.

YOU WILL NEED
Pencil
Tracing paper
25 cm × 115 cm (¼ yd × 45 in) fabric
25 cm × 90 cm (¼ yd × 36 in) thick wadding (batting)
25 cm × 115 cm (¼ yd × 45 in) lining fabric
Scissors
Pins
Needle and thread
Bias binding for edge and loop

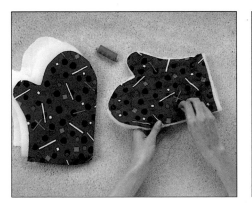

1 Scale up and trace the templates, then cut out one fabric front, one wadding (batting) and one lining piece for each shape. As the quilting will make the glove shrink a little, leave an extra 12 mm (½ in) seam allowance. Pin and tack together one front, wadding (batting) and lining. Repeat with the other. Quilt in vertical lines.

2 Place the pattern on the glove and trim neatly leaving 6 mm (¼ in) seam allowance. Make a loop from a strip of bias binding, by folding it in half and sewing the two sides together. Pin the loop to one side of the glove wrist.

3 Place the two sides of the glove right sides together. Pin, tack and sew. Zigzag around the edges to neaten and turn through. Cut a piece of bias binding slightly larger than the glove wrist. Pin horizontally, then tack and sew in place.

TISSUE HOLDER

A pretty tissue holder looks attractive on a bedside table or dressing table. This one is small enough to carry around in a little bag or purse.

YOU WILL NEED

28 cm (11 in) lace trimming
Scissors
Pins
16.5 cm × 14 cm (6½ in × 5½ in) satin, or to fit small tissue packet
16.5 cm × 14 cm (6½ in × 5½ in) cotton lining
Needle and thread
Iron
Packet of tissues
Ribbon roses

1 Cut the lace into two equal lengths and pin them along the two short sides of the satin on the right side.

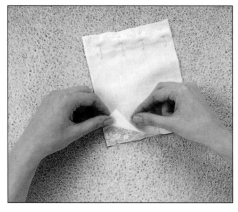

2 Place the cotton lining on top, pin, tack and sew along the two short sides. Turn through and press.

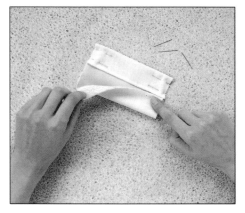

3 Mark the centre of each long side with a pinch mark in the fabric, then fold the two short sides inwards to meet in the centre. Machine sew the two open sides. Trim each corner diagonally, zigzag to neaten, then turn through. To finish, insert a packet of tissues and sew pretty ribbon roses at the opening.

PARTY BIB

The rocking-horse and bird motifs on this little bib make it equally suitable for either a baby boy or a baby girl. Just right for a celebration tea party.

YOU WILL NEED
Tracing paper
Felt-tip pen
Scissors
30 cm × 115 cm (⅓ yd × 45 in) cotton lawn
30 cm (⅓ yd) flat wadding (batting)
Masking tape
Pencil
Pins
Needle and cotton embroidery thread
Bias binding
Button or velcro spots

1 Draw a bib shape onto tracing paper. Scale up the rocking-horse and bird motif and draw onto tracing paper using a felt-tip pen. Cut out two bib shapes in fabric and one in wadding (batting). Lay the tracing on a white surface and hold in place with masking tape. Centre the bib front over the design and hold the material in place with masking tape. The motif will show through the fabric. Trace the motif onto the bib front using a fine pencil.

2 Pin together the front, wadding (batting) and back, and tack, working from the centre out, one side at a time.

3 Quilt over the design with small running stitches.

4 Pin on the bias binding, right sides together, then tack, fold to the back and slip stitch. Make a fastening with either a thread loop and button, or use velcro spots.

COSY
COAT

Quilt tartan fabric, bind with satin and tie a decorative bow to keep your favourite pooch snug on a winter walk. Measure your dog along the back, around the stomach and chest. You could make a trial pattern from some old sheeting instead of paper.

YOU WILL NEED
Plain paper
Pencil
Scissors
30 cm × 115 cm (⅓ yd × 45 in) tartan fabric
30 cm × 115 cm (⅓ yd × 45 in) wadding (batting)
30 cm × 115 cm (⅓ yd × 45 in) lining
Pins
Needle and thread
Velcro fastenings
Satin bias binding
Satin ribbon

1 Using the template as a guide, scale up and cut out paper patterns for the right and left sides. Place on the tartan fabric and cut out, making sure that the tartan lines will match across the centre back seam. Cut out the wadding (batting) and lining slightly larger using the pattern as a guide. Pin and tack the top, wadding (batting) and lining together. Quilt along the tartan.

2 Lay on the patterns once again and trim.

3 Sew the velcro fastenings on the stomach piece.

4 Join the two side pieces together along the back. Pin and sew on the bias binding.

5 Make a bow out of satin ribbon, and sew onto the front together with the velcro fastenings for the chest.

QUILTED PLACE MATS

A set of place mats adds an elegant touch to a family supper or celebration dinner party. Different fabrics will suit a variety of occasions and the mats can be made from colourful remnants or leftover pieces in the same design as your soft furnishing scheme. The quantities given here are sufficient for four mats, but if you have more fabric, you can make a larger number.

YOU WILL NEED

4 pieces of interfacing, 33 cm × 28 cm
    (13 in × 11 in)
4 pieces of plain cotton backing fabric,
    37 cm × 32 cm (14½ in × 12½ in)
Pins
Scissors
Needle and thread
4 pieces of patterned cotton fabric,
    33 cm × 28 cm (13 in × 11 in)
Masking tape

1 Pin a piece of the interfacing in the centre of a piece of the backing fabric leaving a border of 20 mm (¾ in) all the way round. Trim the corners of the backing fabric diagonally to allow a neat turnover. Tack (baste) the interfacing in place and remove the pins. Repeat with the remaining pieces of fabric.

2 Turn over the borders of the backing fabric of each place mat, pin in position and tack (baste) down. To make the corners neat, turn the raw edges under before folding down.

3 Place the patterned fabric pieces on top of the interfacing, leaving an equal border all round. Pin and tack (baste) in place.

4 Starting at one corner, lay down a diagonal strip of masking tape as a guideline for the quilting. Tear off a smaller strip of tape and place it next to the first strip. This strip serves as a gauge for the amount of space to be left between the long pieces of tape. Move it along as you lay down these long pieces. Be careful not to overlap the strips as the channel between them is the guide for the stitching. Sew along the edges of the tape. Repeat on the other diagonal to create quilted diamonds. Fold over 12 mm (½ in) of backing fabric, tuck the edge under and sew along the border several times to finish.

Choosing fabrics for patchwork

Many fabrics are suitable for patchwork, providing they are reasonably firm and do not stretch. A lightweight, pure cotton is probably the best type to use as it will cut and sew well without fraying too badly; patchwork made from cotton can be pressed easily to form crisp flat seams. Use a pure cotton thread for sewing rather than a polyester/cotton blend as this may, in time, wear away the edges of the fabric. When making patchwork avoid furnishing fabrics as these are too thick to handle successfully; knits, stretch fabrics and those with a pile such as velvet are also difficult to use.

Using templates

When using templates cut from template plastic or card, mark the template with the seam allowance, straight grain and other relevant information. Paper templates do not have the seam allowance included, so you must allow for this when cutting out your patches.

Straight grain

The term 'straight grain' refers to the fabric threads running from top to bottom in a piece of fabric (the warp) and from side to side (the weft). When cutting out fabric, always align the straight grain marked on your template with the straight grain of the fabric to minimize distortion when joining the patches.

Using fusible bonding paper

Trace the design elements onto a piece of fusible bonding paper. Cut the paper into separate shapes, then place on the wrong side of your fabric, making sure the adhesive side of the paper is face down. Press in place, setting the iron to the correct temperature for the fabric. Allow to cool, then cut out the shapes (*left*). Lay them in position on the background, adhesive side down, and carefully press with a warm iron.

Machine stitching

Always work a practice piece before starting to stitch to check that your thread, needle, stitch size and fabric are compatible. Fit a new needle before starting as a blunt one will damage the fabric and may result in uneven stitching.

Applying bias binding

Pin the bias binding on the right side of the fabric with right sides facing and raw edges aligning (*above*). Tack (baste) and stitch in position with a 6 mm (¼ in) seam allowance. Remove the tacking (basting) stitches, turn the free edge of the binding over to the wrong side of the fabric and slip stitch with matching thread to secure in place.

Whip stitch

Use whip stitch for joining patchwork shapes when they are tacked (basted) over paper templates. Work the stitches evenly and try to keep them as small as possible.

Place two shapes together with right sides together and the edges aligning. Work whip stitch over the two edges, working steadily from right to left.

Slip stitch

Use slip stitch for joining two folded fabric edges together or when securing bias binding. When joining two folds, the stitches are almost invisible and are worked from the right side. Place the two folded edges together with right sides facing you, slip the needle along inside the fold of one edge, take the needle across to the other edge and slip it along that fold.

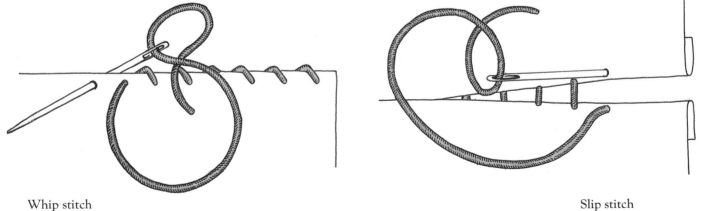

Whip stitch   Slip stitch

NOTICE BOARD

Postcards, messages and lists can be displayed on this colourful cheerful patchwork notice board. It is easily made and is light enough to be hung using self-adhesive velcro spots.

YOU WILL NEED

25 cm × 115 cm (¼ yd × 45 in)
    cotton fabric in 4 different colours
Tape measure
Scissors
Pins
Sewing thread
Steam iron
50 cm (½ yd) black fabric
Velcro spots
60 cm (24 in) square of polystyrene
    (styrofoam) board 2.5 cm (1 in)
    thick
Map pins
Narrow black ribbon
Drawing pins (thumb tacks)

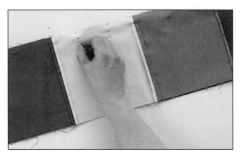

1 Cut out four 16.5 cm (6½ in) squares from each of the four colours of fabric.

2 Lay out the squares in the chosen order. Sew the squares together first in pairs, then in fours, and finally in rows. Check the squares and press after each addition.

3 When all the squares are joined, measure two opposite sides and cut out a 10 cm (4 in) wide piece of black fabric to fit. Pin and sew, then press. Repeat for the remaining two sides. Press well.

4 Stick the velcro spots in place on the polystyrene. Lay the patchwork wrong side up on a flat surface. Place the polystyrene board over it, centring over the patches. Wrap the black bands around, holding in place with map pins. Fold the corners neatly and secure with more map pins.

5 On the right side, pin lengths of black ribbon, folding under the ends, to form a diamond lattice design. Where they cross each other, secure with drawing pins (thumb tacks).

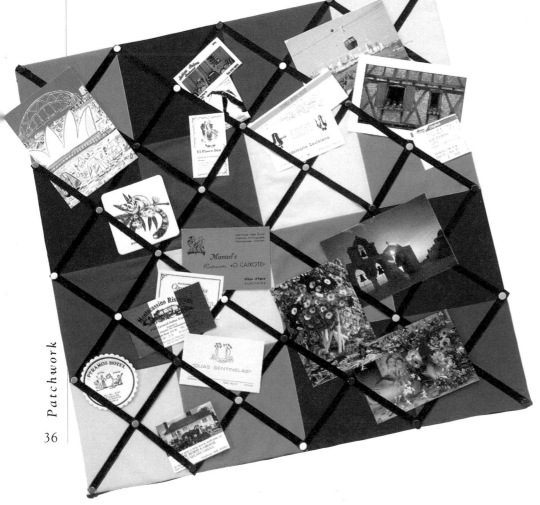

SUFFOLK PUFF EARRINGS

Handmade earrings are always interesting, and the Suffolk Puff patchwork technique lends itself well to these beaded silk beauties.

YOU WILL NEED
Card
Pair of compasses
Pencil
Pair of felt-covered earring bases
15 cm × 7.5 cm (6 in × 3 in) green silk
Fray check liquid
Scissors
Needle and thread
Tiny piece of pink satin
Pink beads

1 Make a circular template in card twice the size of the earring base and draw around it onto the green silk. Apply fray check liquid over this line. When it is dry, cut out the fabric.

2 Turn in a narrow hem and run a gathering stitch around the circle.

3 Draw up the gathering stitch thread, so that the circle puffs, insert a small piece of satin into the centre, then tie a knot to finish off. Slip stitch the puff onto the earring base, making sure it is in the centre.

4 Sew tiny beads all along the edge. Repeat the steps to make the other earring.

SCENTED SACHETS

These little patchwork sachets are made to appear gift-wrapped by using the Seminole patchwork technique. They are quick to make in batches of six. Filled with pot-pourri they give a delicate fragrance when tucked into drawers.

YOU WILL NEED

25 cm × 115 cm (¼ yd × 45 in) *patterned fabric (to make 6 sachets)*

25 cm × 115 cm (¼ yd × 45 in) *plain fabric (to make 6 sachets)*

Scissors

Pins

Needle and thread

Iron

Patchwork square rule or set (T) square

Pot-pourri

Wadding (batting)

Pinking shears

1 Cut out two strips 45 cm × 6.5 cm (18 in × 2½ in) of the patterned fabric and three strips 45 cm × 2.5 cm (18 in × 1 in) of the plain fabric. Cut out six pieces 12.5 cm × 7.5 cm (5 in × 3 in) of the plain fabric for the backing. Sew the two wide strips on either side of one of the narrow strips, and press seams open flat.

2 Straighten the ends with a patchwork square rule or set square to make each sachet. Measure and cut out two 4 cm (1½ in) strips down the joined strip.

3 Cut out a 12.5 cm (5 in) piece from one of the plain fabric strips. Pin, then sew this between the two joined strips, so that a cross of plain fabric is made. Press.

4 Place the backing piece and front right sides together, pin and sew around three sides of the sachet. Trim the corners diagonally, then turn through and press.

5 Fill the sachet with pot-pourri and wadding (batting). Slip stitch to close. Using pinking shears, cut a narrow strip of the plain fabric, tie into a bow and sew on top.

PIN CUSHION

Triangles of black and white striped fabric are joined together to make this hexagonal pin cushion with an effective chevron design. This simple technique is known as English patchwork. Spotted fabric has been used on the back.

YOU WILL NEED

Pencil
Template plastic or card
Scissors
Stiff paper
30 cm × 10 cm (12 in × 4 in) striped fabric
30 cm × 10 cm (12 in × 4 in) spotted fabric
Pins
Needle and thread
Iron
Wadding (batting)

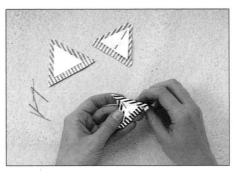

2 Fold one of the paper templates in half, open and place on the wrong side of one of the striped triangles. Make sure the folded line runs along a stripe. Pin, then fold over the seam allowance and tack (baste) through the paper. Continue until you have six striped and six spotted pieces.

3 To join the triangles, place the triangles right sides together and match up the stripes. Using a small fine needle, whip stitch the triangles together until you have made two hexagons. Press.

4 Place the hexagons right sides together and whip stitch around the edge, leaving a gap for stuffing. Gently snip the tacking stitches and remove the papers. Turn through and stuff with wadding (batting) until firm.

5 Slip stitch to close.

1 Draw an equilateral triangle onto template plastic or card and cut out. Check that the triangle is accurate by placing it on paper and drawing round it once, then turning it around to make sure it fits whichever way it is placed. There is no seam allowance. Draw around the pattern 12 times onto stiff paper and cut out the triangles. Draw around the template six times onto the wrong side of the striped fabric and six times onto the spotted fabric, allowing 6 mm (¼ in) seam allowance between each triangle. Make sure that one stripe runs from the top point to the base of each triangle. Cut out.

HEART WALLHANGING

This striking design is made very economically from small pieces of calico, each appliquéd with a different patterned fabric heart. The pieces are sewn together to make a complete picture, and then finished off with a fabric border.

YOU WILL NEED
Drawing paper
Pencil
Scissors
Pins
Remnants of patterned fabric
Pieces of calico
Steam iron
Needle and thread

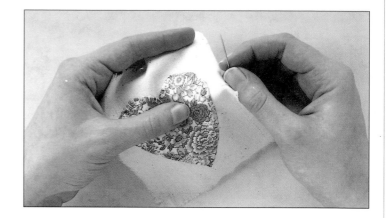

1 Make a heart-shaped template and pin onto a scrap of printed fabric. Draw round the template and cut out adding a border of 6 mm (¼ in) all the way round for the seam allowance. Repeat with the other scraps of patterned fabric. Cut out large enough rectangles of calico for the hearts to have a surrounding border. Press each fabric piece flat and then turn the seam allowance under. Pin each heart shape onto a calico rectangle and sew into position using either an overcast or running stitch.

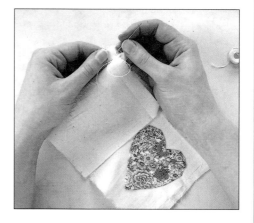

2 Arrange the pieces in a pleasing pattern and sew the rectangles together in rows turning the edges under. Cut a bias strip of patterned fabric about 5 cm (2 in) wide for the border and sew into place.

COT QUILT

This original cot quilt with colourful patchwork blocks and binding would make a beautiful gift for a new-born baby. You could add a label embroidered with the baby's name and date of birth.

YOU WILL NEED

1.5 m × 115 cm (1½ yd × 45 in) spotted fabric

25 cm (¼ yd) each of 4 contrasting fabrics

70 cm × 90 cm (¾ yd × 36 in) wadding (batting)

70 cm × 115 cm (¾ yd × 45 in) backing fabric

Ruler

Rotary mat and cutter or scissors

Pins

Needle and thread

Iron

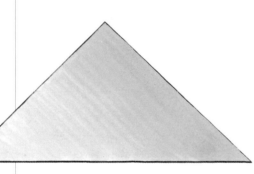

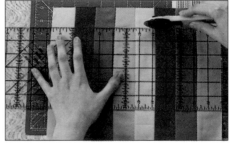

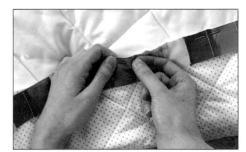

1 Cut out two lengths 90 cm × 14 cm (36 in × 5½ in), four lengths 40 cm × 14 cm (15½ in × 5½ in) and three squares 14 cm (5½ in) of the spotted fabric. Using the template, cut out six triangles from each of the contrasting fabrics and 24 from the spotted fabric. The template and measurements include a 6 mm (¼ in) seam allowance. Join the contrasting fabric triangles together to form squares, first pinning then sewing, checking and pressing before each stage. Add a spotted triangle on each side of these squares to form diamond shapes.

2 Join the three spotted squares to the patched squares, so there is a spotted square on either side. This forms the centre strip. Next join two patched squares at either end of one of the shorter lengths of spotted fabric. Repeat so that these two lengths fit either side of the centre strip, with the three spotted squares. Join them together and press. Join the two remaining medium spotted strips to the top and bottom of the quilt centre. Finally join the two long spotted strips on either side of the quilt. The quilt should now measure 90 cm × 65 cm (36 in × 25½ in).

3 Tack together the top, wadding (batting) and backing fabric. Machine or hand quilt, making sure that the quilting lines are no further than 10 cm (4 in) apart. Trim the edges neatly.

4 To make the binding, cut two 45 cm × 5 cm (18 in × 2 in) strips of each contrasting colour fabric, and join them together to make a piece 45 cm × 32 cm (18 in × 12 in). Cut across these strips as shown, then join to make the binding, about 300 cm (120 in) long.

5 Pin the binding in place at the top and bottom with the right sides together, and sew. Attach the binding to the sides in the same way. Fold over to the back and slip stitch in place.

FESTIVE TABLE MAT

This festive table mat can be used year after year until it becomes a family heirloom. It could also be used as a wall hanging. The design is based on two squares which rotate to form triangles. The larger of the triangles are strip-patched with Christmassy co-ordinating fabrics. A rotary cutter and self-healing board speed up cutting strip patches.

YOU WILL NEED
Pencil
Template plastic
Craft knife or rotary cutter
Ruler
Scissors
Assorted festive and co-ordinating fabrics
Pins
Needle and thread
Steam iron
Heavy vilene

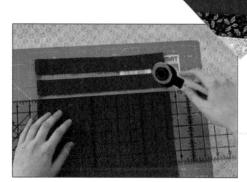

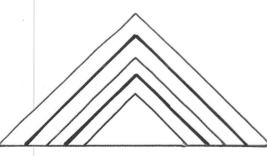

1 Scale up and trace the templates onto plastic. There is no seam allowance so draw round them and use the edges as a stitching guide. Cut out strips of fabric 4 cm (1½ in) wide. The larger triangles will require six strips, the smaller four.

2 Pin, tack (baste) and sew the strips in pairs, right sides together, chain-style, leaving a seam allowance of 6 mm (¼ in). Press the seams flat and join in pairs again to produce a large striped panel.

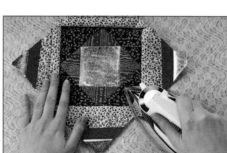

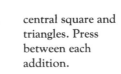

3 Place the templates on the back of the joined strips and cut out leaving a seam allowance of 6 mm (¼ in) between each triangle.

4 Working from the centre out join on all the components, including the central square and triangles. Press between each addition.

5 When the mat is completed, cut a piece of vilene to fit. Turn the seam allowance over and slip stitch into place. A further backing may be sewn on if you wish.

GREETINGS CARD

Needle and thread are not necessary for making this ingenious patchwork greetings card. As only very small pieces of fabric are needed, many combinations can be achieved by merely using scraps.

YOU WILL NEED
Pencil
Fusible iron-on bonding paper
Three-fold greetings card with cut-out
   aperture
Steam iron
Small pieces of three contrasting
   fabrics
Narrow double-sided tape

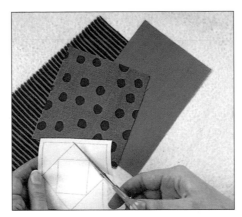

1 Draw your patchwork design onto fusible bonding paper. Making sure the three-fold card is the right way up, outline the square in pencil as a guide.

2 Cut up the bonding paper and place the pieces of the design in separate heaps. Using a steam iron, press the shapes onto the reverse side of the chosen contrasting fabrics.

3 Cut out the shapes carefully and peel off the backing paper from all the pieces. Arrange them within the square on the card to form a block. Press gently with a warm steam iron.

4 Put double-sided tape around the aperture and the card edges, then peel off the backing paper. Close the card carefully, smoothing from the folded side outwards.

PAINTED SILK SCARF

Freehand painting on silk gives a beautiful effect as the colours merge and shine on the fabric. Experiment with designs to suit favourite outfits, or paint matching ones for a family group. Silk paints can be found in most craft or art supply shops.

YOU WILL NEED
Hemmed natural silk square
Pins
Old picture frame
Pen
Paper
Silk outliner (gutta)
Non-toxic silk dyes in an assortment of colours
Soft paintbrushes
Sponge
Iron

1 Stretch the silk square by pinning it onto an old picture frame. Sketch out your design on paper, and draw the outline onto the silk using the silk outliner (gutta). This prevents the colours from running.

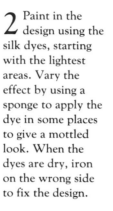 **2** Paint in the design using the silk dyes, starting with the lightest areas. Vary the effect by using a sponge to apply the dye in some places to give a mottled look. When the dyes are dry, iron on the wrong side to fix the design.

PRESERVE JAR COVERS

Homemade preserves are a delight on any breakfast table and look even more tempting with these traditional cotton covers. The design can be adapted according to the type of preserve: try oranges, raspberries or blueberries, as well as that old favourite – strawberries.

YOU WILL NEED
Plate
Pencil
Remnants of gingham or printed cotton
Pinking shears
Scissors
Coloured felt
Rubber-based adhesive
Black fabric pen
Elastic band
Narrow red ribbon

1 Using a plate about 7.5 cm (3 in) wider than the jar lid, draw a circle on the wrong side of the fabric. Cut out using pinking shears. Cut out strawberry shapes and green leaves from the felt.

2 Stick the strawberries and leaves onto the central area of the fabric using rubber-based adhesive.

3 Carefully mark the pips on the fruit using a black fabric pen.

4 Place the cover on the jar and secure with an elastic band. Finish by tying a piece of red ribbon into a neat bow.

T-SHIRT

Give your plain white T-shirt a new lease of life with this striking tulip design. Why not wear your art on your sleeve, chest or back?

YOU WILL NEED
White T-shirt
Steam iron
Piece of cardboard
Green, red and brown fabric paints
Small paintbrush

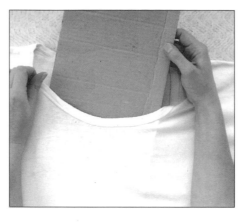

1 Iron the T-shirt and slip a piece of cardboard inside it so that the paint will not seep through to the back. Make sure the T-shirt is quite flat by smoothing it out with your hands.

2 Start the design using green fabric paints, painting the green stalks first. Next paint the red tulips, extending them slightly around the neck to emphasize the shape. Draw an outline of brown fabric paint with the brush to enhance and define the design. Iron the T-shirt to fix the fabric paint.

HAIR SCRUNCHY

Scraps of pretty fabric can be used to make hair ornaments. Try to match a special outfit for a party or birthday outing.

YOU WILL NEED
20 cm × 14 cm (8 in × 5½ in) satin
  fabric
Pins
Needle and thread
15 cm (6 in) narrow elastic

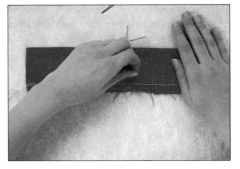

1 With the right sides together, fold the fabric in half lengthways. Pin together, allowing 10 mm (⅜ in) for the seam, and stitch.

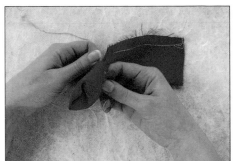

2 Press the seam open and turn through to the right side.

3 Thread the elastic through the fabric tube and stitch one end securely.

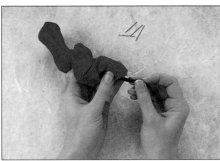

4 Gather the fabric along the length of the elastic until it forms a 'scrunched' shape.

5 Turn under 10 mm (⅜ in) of fabric at one end. Sew together the ends of the elastic and slip stitch the ends of the fabric together securely.

WILD BEAST NAPKIN RINGS

Give your dinner guests something to talk about by making these unusual felt napkin rings. Not only do these wild beasts look good chasing their tails around a napkin, but when everyone unwraps their napkins, the beasts will look great racing each other around the table!

YOU WILL NEED

For each napkin ring:
Pencil
Thin card
Scissors
18 cm × 14 cm (7 in × 5½ in)
    coloured felt
Small amounts of black and white felt
Needle and thread
Small press-stud (snap fastener)

1 Draw an animal shape on thin card. Cut out and place it on the coloured felt. Draw around the shape and cut out the animal.

2 Cut out a small white felt circle and a smaller black felt circle for the eye, and sew into place.

3 Sew the press-stud (snap fastener) halves in place on the nose and bottom of the animals. Fasten around the napkin.

CUSTOMIZED SHOES

Use fabric pens for a great way of brightening up a pair of inexpensive fabric shoes and giving them a 'designer' look.

YOU WILL NEED
Pair of fabric shoes in a plain colour
Newspaper
Fabric pens with fine and thick tips
Assorted glitter inks and expanding
*   fabric paints*

1 Stuff the shoes with news-paper. Draw zig-zags on the sides of the shoes, and some pink spirals all over the front of the shoes.

2 Using silver glitter ink, add zigzags and dots.

3 Dot around the edges of the shoes with expanding fabric paint. Leave to dry.

MILLION-DOLLAR HAT

Buy lots of inexpensive ribbon and ready-made rosebuds and make an old straw hat look like a million dollars for a special occasion.

YOU WILL NEED
Assortment of wide and narrow satin ribbons
Scissors
Straw hat
Strong clear glue
Needle and wide thread
Satin ribbon rosebuds

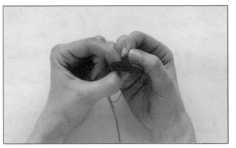

1 Cut a long piece of wide ribbon for the main band. Cut long pieces of narrow ribbon to place around the hat and shorter pieces of wide ribbon to make rosebuds. Glue the long piece of ribbon around the hat.

2 Using a shorter piece of wide ribbon, start at one end and roll it loosely until it forms a coil. Then gripping the coil at the bottom, sew it together to secure the shape of a rosebud.

3 For the leaf, fold a shorter piece of wide green ribbon, so that the two ends meet halfway across the middle. Stick this seam together with glue. Place the rosebuds over the seams on the leaf and glue them together. Leave to dry, then secure even further with one or two stitches. Make as many rosebuds as you require in lots of different colours and sizes.

4 Place the rosebud stems mainly at the back of the hat in a cluster to hide the meeting points of the ribbon glued around the hat. Then place the little ready-made rosebuds around the brim of the hat in a semi-ordered fashion. Secure these with one or two little stitches through the straw of the hat.

TIE-DYED SCARF

The technique of tie-dying is very simple to master. You can easily produce stunning artistic effects by altering the pattern of knots and colours.

YOU WILL NEED
Needle and thread
Pre-hemmed square of natural white silk
Scissors
Cotton string or raffia
Rubber gloves
Cold or hot dyes, in 2 colours
Bucket or stainless steel pan
Spoon for stirring

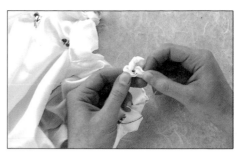

1 Pass the needle and thread through the silk square, and pull and twist the thread around tightly until you have a tight little 'peak' at least 20 mm (¾ in) long. Knot the thread and cut the end. Make at least 15 little peaks in the same way, scattered over the scarf.

2 Fold the silk over into a triangle, and make two tight knots at each corner.

3 Fold over once more to form a smaller triangle. Hold the fabric in the centre and bring the two ends together. Criss-cross the string over the silk until you almost reach the knotted corners. Tie the string securely.

4 Wearing rubber gloves, prepare the first dye in a bucket or stainless steel pan following the manufacturer's instructions. When the dye is ready for use, immerse the knotted silk scarf stirring occasionally. Cold dyes require 60 minutes, hot dyes 10–15 minutes. Then remove the scarf and rinse it under cold water until this runs clear.

5 Untie the cord binding and the knots at the corners of the silk. Unfold the scarf, leaving the little peaks. Refold in the opposite direction so that the corners of the triangle which were double become single and vice versa. Knot each corner three times. Holding the middle of the longest side, twist and knot two or three times until you reach the knotted corners of the scarf.

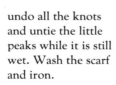

6 Prepare the second dye as before and proceed in the same way. When the silk is thoroughly rinsed, undo all the knots and untie the little peaks while it is still wet. Wash the scarf and iron.

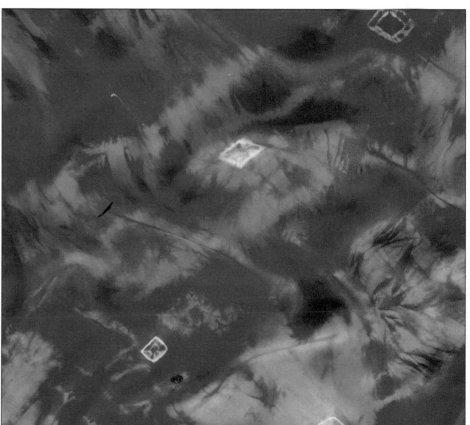

KNOTTED
HAIRBAND

You can make this unusual hairband with a variety of coloured ribbons, and even produce a series to co-ordinate with different outfits or for special occasions.

YOU WILL NEED
Pins
Cushion pad
2 m (2 yd) lengths of 3 mm (⅛ in) wide ribbons in 6 colours
Wide elastic
Needle and thread

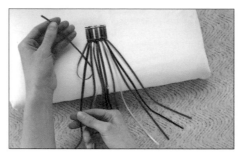

1 Starting with two ribbons of the same colour in the middle, pin the ribbons on the cushion pad. Pin the other ribbons to the left and right of the central pair so that the colours on the left reflect those on the right. Place another row of pins 2.5 cm (1 in) down from the first row. Following diagram 1, begin knotting with the first ribbon on the left, working across to the right until you reach the centre point.

3 Next divide the 12 ribbons into four groups of three. Braid in the conventional way to produce four braids 4 cm (1½ in) long.

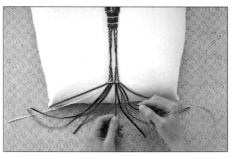

2 Now knot from the first ribbon on the right side following the knotting technique shown in diagram 2. Continue knotting from both sides to the centre for 14 rows.

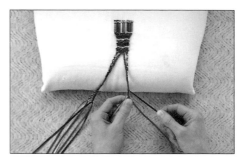

4 Divide the braids into two bunches and wrap one bunch tightly with one of the ribbons. Repeat with the other bunch. Swop the colours and continue wrapping for 5 cm (2 in). Divide the ribbons again into braiding groups and continue braiding and wrapping until you have the desired length.

5 Pin and knot the ends of the ribbons and cut off any excess.

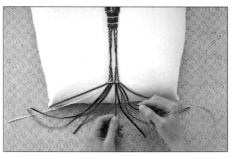

6 Stitch a short length of wide elastic to the ribbon knots, passing the thread through the knots to secure.

RIBBON
WREATH

This charming variation on the traditional festive wreath is perfect for hanging on a room door or on the wall. It is not suitable for a front door as rain would spoil the paper.

YOU WILL NEED
2 lengths of red paper ribbon, 8 cm
    (3¼ in) wide
Scissors
Roll of green crepe paper 2.5 m
    (2½ yd) long
Reel of copper wire
Wire cutters
Strong clear glue
2 m × 12 mm (2 yd × ½ in) gold
    ribbon
Awl
2 m × 12 mm (2 yd × ½ in) green
    ribbon
2 m × 20 mm (2 yd × ¾ in) red satin
    ribbon
2 m × 20 mm (2 yd × ¾ in) green
    satin ribbon
Artificial red berries mounted on wire

1 Concertina one length of the red paper ribbon into 7 cm (2¾ in) folds. With the ribbon folded cut zig-zag shapes at the top and bottom. Cut a long strip of green crepe paper 20 cm (8 in) wide. Fold in half lengthways and cut out feathery shapes 5 cm (2 in) deep on the top and bottom.

2 Unfold the red paper ribbon. Lay the copper wire along the centre lengthways and cut the wire to this length. Draw a line of glue along the centre of the red paper ribbon. Place the copper wire on this. Cut a matching length of gold ribbon and stick over the copper wire, making sure it also sticks to the red paper.

3 Unfold the green crepe paper and line it with the second length of red paper ribbon. Lay on a flat surface with the red uppermost, and place the red paper strip with the gold ribbon at right angles on top. Hold down firmly. Fold the green crepe paper strip over the red paper strip at right angles. Repeat this process in the opposite direction until the strips are completely over each other.

4 Hold the folded paper together and using an awl, pierce two holes 2.5 cm (1 in) apart in the centre, piercing through all the layers at once. Twist two strands of copper wire together to make 2 × 60 cm (2 ft) lengths of stronger wire. Thread the twisted wire strands through the holes and fasten the ends together to form a circle. Open the concertina gently to create a wreath.

5 Decorate by twisting berries and ribbons over and under the gaps, using the wires to hold them in place.

CHRISTMAS BALLET SHOES

Transform a pair of ballet shoes to wear at a Christmas party by decorating them with brightly coloured berries and ribbons. For this pair, ribbon with a floating thread at the back was gathered up the centre.

YOU WILL NEED
Pair of ballet shoes
Artificial holly berries
Needle and thread
20 cm (8 in) narrow metallic ribbon
Ribbon with floating thread, four
   times the length of each shoe

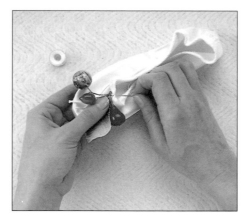

1 For each shoe, bind some berries together, and sew onto the fronts of the shoes.

2 Cut the length of metallic ribbon in half. Form three loops in each piece, with the largest loop at the bottom. Sew the loops over the berries.

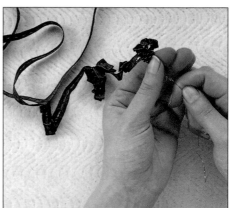

3 Gather the ribbon to fit round each shoe by pulling on the floating thread.

4 Sew the ribbon in position around the top of the shoe. Finish with a twirl at the front to cover and obscure the points where the loops and berries join the shoe.

HAIR CLIP

Disguise a plain hair clip with a pretty ribbon bow to match your dress.

YOU WILL NEED
21 cm (8½ in) length of ribbon
6 cm (2¼ in) length of ribbon
Needle and thread
Plain hair clip

1 Fold the ends of the longer piece of ribbon inwards to meet in the centre and sew them together. Leave the thread long.

2 Pull on the thread to gather the join.

3 Wrap the shorter piece of ribbon over the join.

4 Sew the ends together at the back and sew the bow onto the clip.

ROSETTE EARRINGS

These unusual clip-on earrings, quickly made with coiled ribbon, can also be used to decorate a pair of shoes.

YOU WILL NEED
1 m (1 yd) wide ribbon
Needle and thread
Pair of clip-on earring backs

1 Cut the length of ribbon in half and use one piece for each earring. Sew a line of running stitches down the centre of the ribbon.

2 Gather the stitches up evenly and coil the ribbon around itself. Secure the coil with a few running stitches.

3 Sew the coil onto the back of each earring.

RIBBON PURSE

This ribbon creation uses simple techniques practised by weavers over the centuries. By interlacing lengths of silk ribbon you can make a pretty purse in no time.

YOU WILL NEED

Double-sided tape
Empty tissue box
Assortment of coloured silk ribbons including black, of different widths, each 1.5 m (60 in) long
Tapestry needle
Small rectangle of self-adhesive black felt
Tailor's chalk
Scissors
Pins
Small rectangle of black cotton satin
Needle and thread
2 black glass buttons
Short length of round black elastic

1 Stick double-sided tape all around the upper part on the sides of the box. Peel off the protective backing. Fix one end of a length of ribbon onto the tape and cross the ribbon over to the other side of the box. Stretch it lightly, fix the end onto the tape and trim. Repeat until the whole box is covered, taking care that the pieces do not overlap. The weft is now ready.

2 Thread a tapestry needle with a length of ribbon. Pass the needle alternately under and over each ribbon of the weft, to the opposite side. Fix the ribbon onto the tape and cut off the remaining ribbon. It might be necessary to push each row of the warp against the previous one with your fingers to get the best results. Repeat to the end.

3 Invert the tissue box and place on the self-adhesive felt. Draw round with tailor's chalk and cut out.

4 Peel off the protective backing and apply sticky-side down onto the ribbons. Press down firmly. Using scissors cut off all the ribbons right round the sides of the box. Trim.

5 Pin the piece of black satin onto the felt, wrong side down. Sew the edges to the felt. Turn inside out.

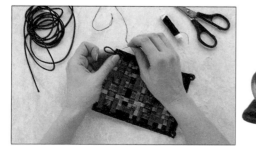

6 Fold the remaining black ribbon in half lengthways and tack (baste) around the purse. Fold the purse in three. Sew the two sides together and sew the ribbon around. Sew on a glass button at each corner of the over-lap. Sew on two loops of elastic.

RIBBON DECORATIONS

There are many different effects that can be achieved by mixing and matching coloured ribbons. They can be plaited or twisted and grouped into colours to cascade down a wrapped present.

YOU WILL NEED
Assortment of ribbons
Scissors
Double-sided tape
Metallic pen

1 One of the most straightforward ways to use ribbon is to curl it. This effect is achieved by pulling the ribbon through closed scissors to make it twist and fall into natural ringlets. Try doing this to different lengths and colours of ribbons and then attach them to your present.

2 Another effective way to use ribbon is to plait it, using at least three different colours. Tape the ribbon ends together and plait to the required length. Secure and cut the ribbon ends.

3 In this example a whole medley of ribbons in different colours and widths is plaited together in order to create a riot of colour. Tape and cut the ribbon ends.

4 To give ribbon an individual look, decorate it by drawing a design taken from the wrapping paper with a metallic pen.

Ribboncrafts

RIBBON WATCHSTRAP

Knot a pretty watchstrap in someone's favourite colours to add a fashionable touch to an everyday timepiece.

YOU WILL NEED
Masking tape
Piece of felt
Pins
Approximately 1.5 m (1½ yd) lengths of 3 mm (⅛ in) ribbon in 5 colours
Watch face
Short length of wide silk ribbon
Needle and thread
Small buckle
Iron

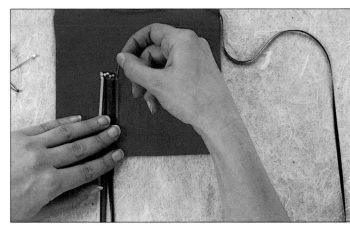

1 Tape the piece of felt to a firm flat surface. Pin the ribbons at one end in a neat row onto the felt. Keep the ribbons flat and pin again 2.5 cm (1 in) down from the first row of pins.

2 Following the diagram, bring each ribbon over, under, and over the one next to it starting with the first ribbon on the left. Continue in this way and knot all the way to the right. The first ribbon on the left will then be the last ribbon on the right.

3 Calculate the circumference of the watch-wearer's wrist. Continue knotting until you reach the halfway point on the strap. Thread the watch onto the ribbon, ensuring the ribbons lie flat across the back. Continue knotting until you reach the required length for the strap.

4 Cover one end of the strap with a small piece of wide silk ribbon and sew it in place on one side. Thread on the buckle and sew down the wide ribbon. Cover the other end of the strap with a piece of wide ribbon and sew in place. Gently stretch the strap and press with a cool iron.

STITCHES

Back stitch

Work back stitch from right to left, making small, even stitches forwards and backwards along the row, keeping the stitches of identical size.

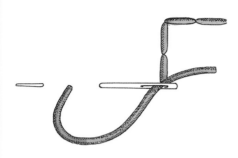

Holbein stitch

This stitch is also known as double running stitch.

Work a row of evenly spaced stitches along the line to be stitched. Fill in the spaces left on the first row with stitches worked on the second row, this time going in the opposite direction.

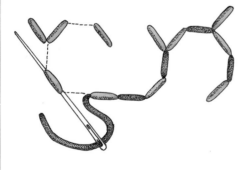

Chain stitch

Work chain stitch downwards by making a series of loops of identical size. Remember to anchor the last loop in the row with a small straight stitch.

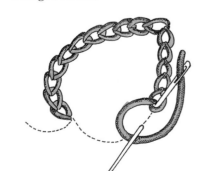

Cross stitch

Begin by working a row of diagonal stitches from right to left, then complete the crosses with a second row of diagonal stitches worked in the opposite direction. Remember that the top diagonal stitches of each cross should always slant in the same direction, usually from bottom left to top right.

Half cross stitch

If you work just the bottom diagonal stitches, the stitch is then called half cross stitch.

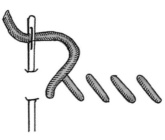

Detached chain stitch

This stitch is also known as daisy stitch or lazy daisy stitch and it is actually a single chain stitch.

Work detached chain stitch in the same way as ordinary chain stitch, but anchor each loop with a small straight stitch before proceeding to make the next loop.

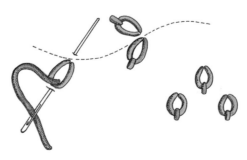

Whipped back stitch

Work whipped back stitch in one or two colours of thread.

First, make a foundation row of ordinary back stitch, making the stitches slightly longer than usual. Using a second thread, whip over the back stitches from right to left, without picking up any fabric. Use a blunt-ended tapestry needle for the second thread to avoid splitting or snagging the stitches on the foundation row.

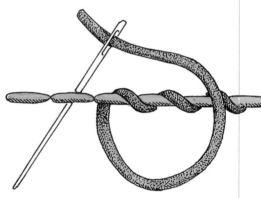

French knot

Bring the thread through the fabric and hold it taut with your left hand. Twist the needle around the thread two or three times, then tighten the twists. Still holding the thread in your left hand, turn the needle and insert it into the fabric at the point where it originally emerged. Pull the needle and thread through the twists to complete the knot.

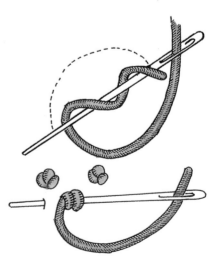

Blanket stitch

Use blanket stitch as an edging stitch for appliqué as well as a surface stitch. You can vary the effect by making the upright stitches alternately long and short or graduate their lengths to form pyramid shapes.

Work blanket stitch from left to right, pulling the needle through the fabric over the top of the working thread. Space the stitches evenly along the row.

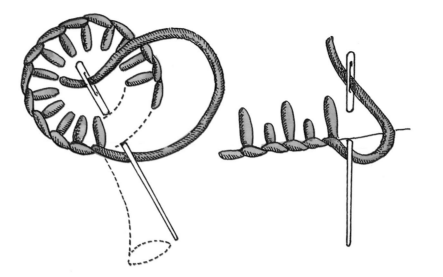

TRANSFERRING A DESIGN

The two easiest ways of transferring a traced design onto a piece of fabric are by using dressmaker's carbon paper or a light source.

Carbon paper

Place a piece of dressmaker's carbon paper with the ink side down on the right side of your fabric. Position the tracing on top, as shown, making sure the design is centred. Pin the layers together round the edge and place on a hard, flat surface. Draw round the outlines with a hard pencil, pressing firmly. Use blue or red carbon paper on light fabric and yellow carbon paper on dark fabric.

Using a light source

This method works well with fine fabric such as cotton or silk. You can use a glass-topped table as shown, or alternatively rest a small sheet of glass or clear plastic between two dining chairs. On a bright, sunny day you can tape both tracing and fabric onto a window and transfer the design in the same way.

Place an adjustable lamp underneath the glass, directing the light upwards. Place the tracing on the glass and secure with masking tape. Position the fabric over the tracing, centring the design, and secure with more tape. Slowly trace the design with a soft, sharp pencil and take care to avoid dragging the fabric as you work.

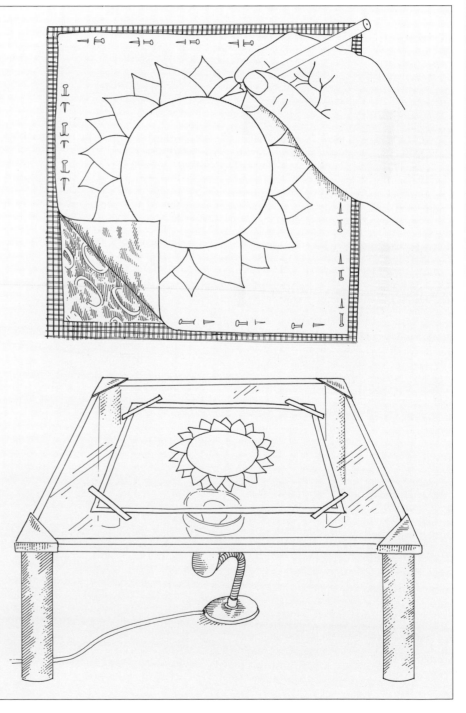

ASSISI BOOKMARK

Assisi embroidery is originally from Italy and it is usually worked in two thread colours on a white or cream background. Here, the technique is used to work a design down the centre of a ready-made fabric bookmark.

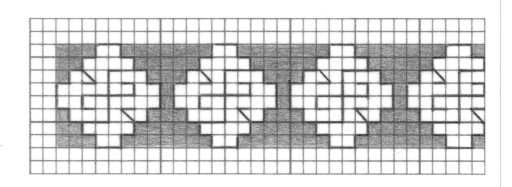

YOU WILL NEED
Ready-made white bookmark with 18-count fabric centre
Stranded cotton in terracotta and dark grey
Tapestry needle

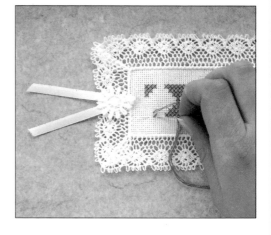

1 Each coloured square on the chart represents one cross stitch worked over two woven blocks in the fabric.

Following the chart, work the background areas in cross stitch using two strands of terracotta thread.

2 Outline the cross stitch areas with Holbein stitch worked over two fabric blocks using two strands of dark grey thread, then work the linear details in the same way.

STITCH SAMPLER GREETINGS CARD

This design gives you the opportunity to practise several embroidery stitches and try out new colour combinations. Arrange the rows of stitches in the form of a sampler and mount your embroidery in a ready-made card.

YOU WILL NEED
*Ready-made cream greetings card
    with an oval aperture*
*Small piece of 18-count ainring in
    lemon yellow*
Water-soluble embroidery marker
*Scraps of stranded cotton in yellow,
    orange, tan, dark red and green or
    any other colour combination*
Tapestry needle
Scissors
Steam iron

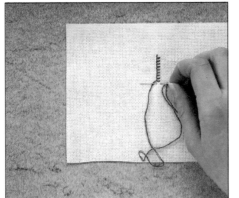

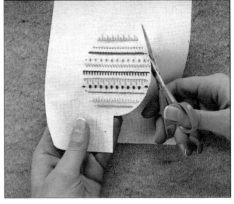

1 Centre the greetings card aperture over the fabric and draw round the oval with the embroidery marker.

2 Fill the oval with horizontal rows of blanket stitch, chain stitch, backstitch, half cross stitch and French knots, making sure you take the ends of each row beyond the oval outline. Use three strands of thread except for the French knots which are worked in six strands.

3 Cut out 6 mm (¼ in) outside the oval outline. Immerse in cold water to remove marker and allow to dry. Press the embroidery on the wrong side with a cool iron and mount in the card following the manufacturer's instructions.

BLACKWORK PAPERWEIGHT

Explore the delicate effect of blackwork, an embroidery technique used throughout Europe since the sixteenth century; by working this design and mounting it in a clear glass paperweight.

YOU WILL NEED
Small piece of 11-count pearl aida fabric in cream
Flower thread in black
Tapestry needle
Square glass craft paperweight
Sharp HB pencil
Scissors

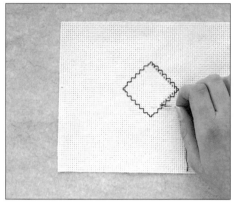

1 Each square on the chart represents one woven block in the fabric. Embroider in Holbein stitch.

2 Remove the card insert from the paperweight and centre it over the embroidery. Draw round the edge of the card with a sharp HB pencil and cut out along the line.

3 Mount the embroidery in the paperweight following the manufacturer's instructions. Finish off the paperweight by pressing the self-adhesive backing in position.

HOLLY GIFT TAG

This holly design is quick to embroider in half cross stitch, adding a bead every time you make a stitch.

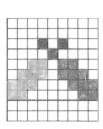

YOU WILL NEED

Scraps of 18-count ainring in white
Stranded cotton in red and two
* shades of green*
Small beads to match each of the
* thread colours*
Tapestry needle
Ready-made cream gift tags
Scissors
Narrow sticky tape
Fine gold cord

1 Each coloured square on the chart represents one half cross stitch worked over two woven blocks in the fabric. Following the chart, work the design using two strands of thread, adding one bead in the appropriate colour with every stitch you make.

2 Centre the holly motif in the gift tag aperture, cut away the surplus fabric and secure with strips of narrow sticky tape.

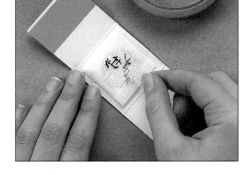

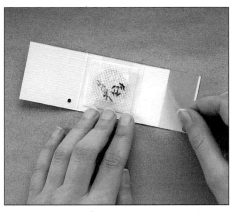

3 Remove the backing strip from the gift tag flap, fold over card and press together with your fingers. Add a loop of fine gold cord and tie the tag on your parcel.

INITIAL KEY RING

Organize your household keys by making each member of the family their own embroidered key ring bearing the appropriate initial.

YOU WILL NEED

Transparent plastic key ring complete with ring
Small piece of bright yellow cotton fabric
Sharp HB pencil
Tracing paper
Stranded cotton in blue
Crewel needle
Steam iron
Medium-weight iron-on interfacing
Scissors

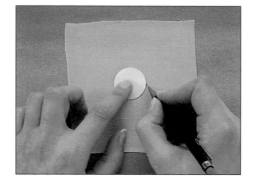

1 Remove the card circle from the key fob and place it on the right side of the fabric. Draw round the card with a sharp HB pencil.

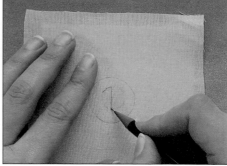

2 Scale up and trace the initial and transfer it to the centre of the card circle using the pencil.

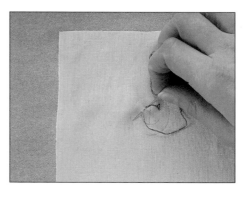

3 Using two strands of blue thread in the crewel needle, embroider the outline of the initial in backstitch, then dot French knots at random over the solid areas.

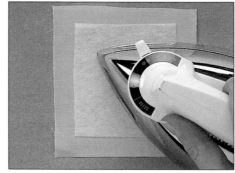

4 Turn the embroidery over and iron a piece of medium-weight iron-on interfacing over the back. Cut out round the drawn circle and mount in the key ring following the manufacturer's instructions.

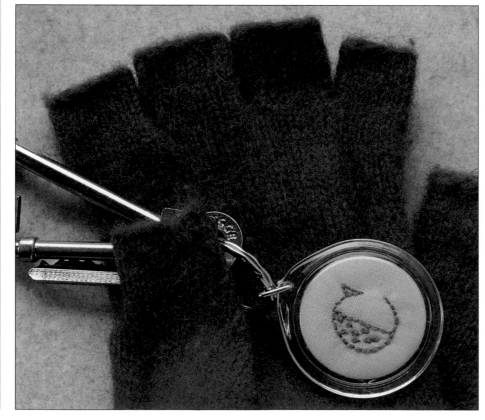

FLORAL PICTURE

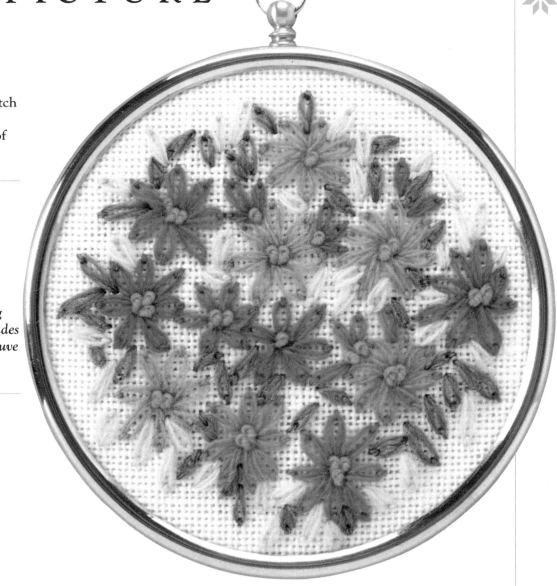

This delightful flower picture is embroidered in detached chain stitch and French knots using an assortment of soft, subtle shades of pink, mauve and green wool.

YOU WILL NEED
Circular brass frame with convex glass
Small piece of white fabric with a fairly open weave
Water-soluble embroidery marker
Steam iron
Medium-weight iron-on interfacing
Zephyr or Persian wool in three shades of pink, two shades of green, mauve and orange
Tapestry needle

1 Place the glass from the frame on the right side of the fabric. Draw round the glass with the marker. Turn the fabric over and iron a piece of medium-weight iron-on interfacing on top.

2 On the right side, mark dots at random inside the circle. Each dot indicates the centre of a flower.

3 Arranging the stitches in a circle round each dot, embroider the flowers in detached chain stitch, using two strands of the pink and mauve wools. Embroider the leaves in detached chain stitch, using two strands of green wool and dotting the stitches at random between the flowers. Finally, fill the centre of each flower with French knots using four strands of orange wool. Mount the embroidery in the frame following the manufacturer's instructions.

BOW HANDKERCHIEF

Embroider this charming bow motif in one corner of a ready-made white handkerchief, perhaps matching the colour of the embroidery to a special outfit.

YOU WILL NEED

Tracing paper
White ready-made cotton or linen
  handkerchief
Water-soluble embroidery marker
Stranded cotton in turquoise
Crewel needle
Steam iron

1 Scale up and trace the bow motif from the template and transfer it to one corner of the handkerchief using the embroidery marker.

2 Embroider the motif in chain stitch using two strands of thread. When the bow is complete, immerse the handkerchief in cold water to remove the embroidery marker outlines and allow to dry. Press on the wrong side with a cool iron.

CHERRY PLACE CARD

Place cards can add a really individual touch to a table setting, whether formal or informal. After the cards have been completed, use a gold felt-tip pen and your best handwriting to add the names.

YOU WILL NEED
Ready-made red place cards with
 aperture
Scraps of white silk or cotton fabric
Sharp HB pencil
Stranded cotton in red and green
Crewel needle
Scissors
Sticky tape

1 Lay the aperture on the place card over the right side of the fabric. Using a sharp HB pencil, mark a dot on the fabric to indicate the centre of each cherry.

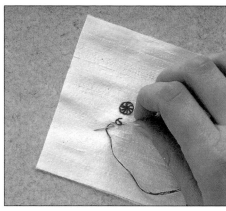

2 Embroider blanket stitch in a circle round each dot using two strands of red thread. Work two lines of backstitch to join the cherries and make the stalks using two strands of green thread.

3 Centre the cherry motif in the place card aperture, cut away the surplus fabric and secure with strips of narrow sticky tape. Remove the backing strip from the place card flap, fold over and press in position.

STITCHES

Jacquard stitch

Work a row of evenly sized diagonal stitches covering three vertical and three horizontal canvas threads. Arrange the stitches in steps of six, as shown. Next, work a row of tent stitches, following the stepped outline. Work alternate rows of the two stitches to fill the shape.

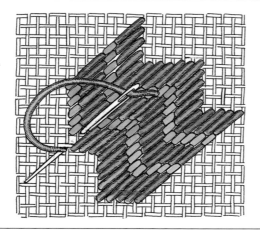

Half cross stitch

Although this stitch looks the same as tent stitch on the right side, the working method for the two stitches is different. These two stitches should not be used on the same piece of needlepoint as they 'pull' and distort the canvas in different directions.

Work rows of small diagonal stitches from top to bottom of the shape, as shown.

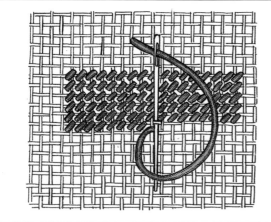

Slanting satin stitch

This versatile stitch can be worked in rows or alternatively stepped to form a zigzag line. It can also be used to embroider small blocks by graduating the lengths of the stitches to fill the corners.

Work diagonal stitches spanning the same number of vertical and horizontal canvas threads, usually two, three or four.

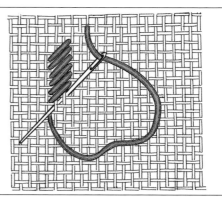

Brighton stitch

Work blocks of five diagonal stitches of graduated length. Arrange the blocks in rows, changing the direction of the slant in alternate rows. Each new row of blocks should be the mirror image of the row above.

After the blocks have been completed, work two straight stitches in a contrasting colour to form an upright cross in the gap between each block.

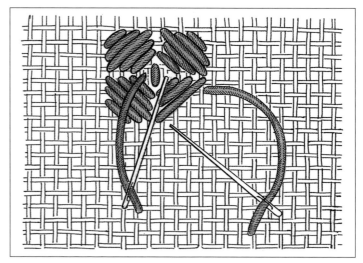

Mosaic stitch

Each mosaic stitch block consists of one diagonal stitch worked over two vertical and two horizontal canvas threads at the centre of two short diagonal stitches. Stitch the blocks individually when embroidering a multicoloured design.

To work background areas in mosaic stitch, work each horizontal row over two journeys. Begin at the top left-hand side and work the first short stitch and the long stitch of each block. On the second journey, complete each block by filling in the remaining short stitch.

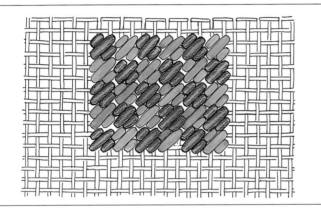

Florentine stitch

Work vertical straight stitches over the required number of horizontal canvas threads, usually four or six, and arrange them in a step sequence to form zigzag rows. Work subsequent rows of stitches in different colours to fill the canvas above and below the first row, following the contours carefully.

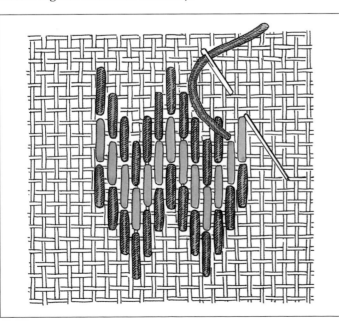

Tent stitch

There are two methods of working tent stitch:

Use the diagonal method shown in the top stitches for working large areas as this method is less likely to pull the canvas out of shape. Work up and down in diagonal rows, making small diagonal stitches over one intersection of the canvas.

Use the second method for embroidering details and single lines. Begin at the lower edge of the shape and work in horizontal rows as shown in the bottom stitches.

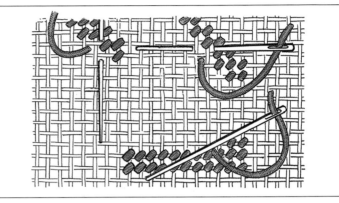

Double Leviathan stitch

Begin by working a large cross over a square of four canvas threads. Work a series of crossing stitches over the top, following the sequence shown in the diagram. Take care to follow the diagrams carefully to achieve the correct result.

BOOKMARK

This bookmark is simple to embroider in Jacquard stitch using nine shades of green thread. You may prefer to use a different colour combination, perhaps one which allows you to use up any oddments of stranded cotton you have.

YOU WILL NEED
Ruler
Small piece of 17-mesh needlepoint canvas
Waterproof black fine felt-tip pen
Stranded cotton in nine shades of green
Tapestry needle
Scissors
Ready-made bookmark with aperture
Sticky tape

1 Mark out a rectangle, slightly larger than the bookmark aperture, on the canvas using a black felt-tip pen.

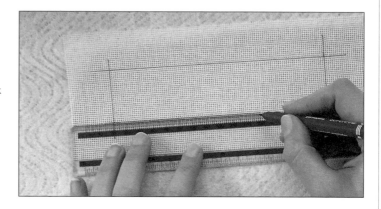

2 Following the chart, cover the rectangle with rows of Jacquard stitch using six strands of cotton. Use eight colours in rotation to stitch the wide rows and the ninth colour to stitch all the narrow rows.

3 Cut out the embroidery leaving a border of 6 mm (¼ in) of unworked canvas all round. Centre the embroidery in the bookmark aperture and secure with narrow sticky tape. Fold over the bookmark and press together with your fingers.

BUTTERFLY
PINCUSHION

Make a needlepoint pincushion decorated with a delicate butterfly motif to keep your pins safe. Make another to give to a friend, choosing a different colour combination.

YOU WILL NEED
Small piece of 17-mesh needlepoint canvas
Stranded cotton in the following colours: 1 skein each of purple, pale blue, kingfisher blue, turquoise and green; 2 skeins of yellow
Tapestry needle
Scissors
Needle and tacking (basting) thread
Small piece of felt to match one of the thread colours
Crewel needle
Polyester stuffing (batting)
Knitting needle
Pinking shears

1 Each coloured square on the chart represents one mosaic stitch. Work the butterfly motif in mosaic stitch using six strands of thread in the tapestry needle.

2 Cut away the surplus canvas round the embroidery leaving a border of 12 mm (½ in). Turn under and tack (baste). Cut out a piece of felt 12 mm (½ in) larger all round than the embroidery. Centre the embroidery on the felt and stitch together with running stitches, using three strands of matching cotton in the crewel needle and leaving a small gap along one side for stuffing the pincushion.

3 Stuff the pincushion using a knitting needle to manoeuvre the stuffing (batting) right into the corners. Sew up the gap, then cut round the felt with pinking shears.

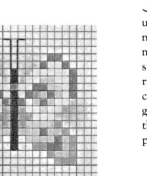

PRETTY NAPKIN RING

Decorate a plain silver- or gold-coloured napkin ring with a strip of perforated paper embroidered with a simple geometric design in half cross stitch.

YOU WILL NEED
Small piece of white perforated paper
Scissors
Plain silver- or gold-coloured napkin ring
Stranded cotton in yellow, blue and turquoise
Tapestry needle
Fabric glue
Small paintbrush
Contact adhesive

1 Cut out a strip of perforated paper large enough to fit round the napkin ring.

2 Each coloured square on the chart represents one half cross stitch. Following the chart, work the design along the paper strip using two strands of thread and leaving both ends of the thread free.

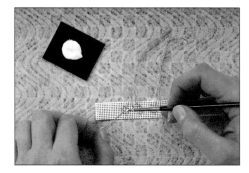

3 Secure the loose threads on the wrong side with a small dab of fabric glue on a paintbrush. Allow to dry, then snip off the thread ends.

4 Using contact adhesive, stick the embroidered strip in place round the napkin ring.

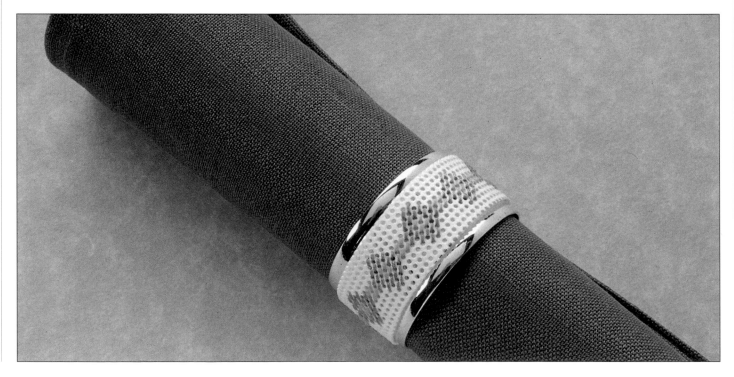

FLORENTINE EVENING BAG

Make this tiny evening bag to hold keys, handkerchief and lipstick on a special night out, co-ordinating the colour scheme with a favourite outfit.

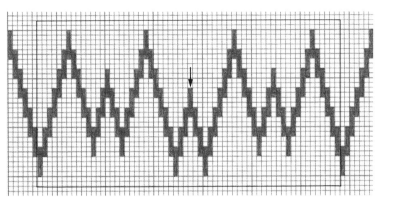

YOU WILL NEED

Ruler

Small piece of 22-mesh needlepoint canvas

Waterproof black fine felt-tip pen

Stranded cotton in the following colours: 2 skeins of purple; 1 skein each of pale blue, blue and kingfisher blue; plus 1 skein to match your fabric colour

Tapestry needle

Metallic-effect silver yarn

Scissors

Sewing needle

Tacking (basting) thread in a contrasting colour

Remnant of heavy silk to match one of the thread colours

Crewel needle

Braid for shoulder strap

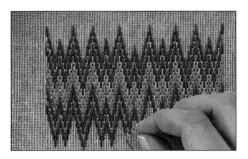

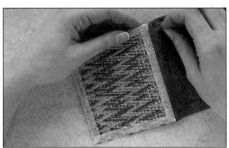

1 Mark out a rectangle 10 cm × 12 cm (4 in × 4¾ in) on the canvas using a black felt-tip pen. Following the chart and beginning at the centre, work one row of Florentine stitch using six strands of the purple thread in the tapestry needle. Work the remaining rows following the zigzag design on the chart. Use six strands of thread throughout, except for the silver yarn which is used singly.

2 Cut out the embroidery leaving a border of 12 mm (½ in) all round. Turn under the raw edges and tack (baste). Cut out a piece of silk 14 × 25 cm (5½ × 10 in), turn under 12 mm (½ in) round the edge and tack (baste). With right sides together, place the embroidery over the silk, matching the edges as shown, and stitch together using two strands of matching thread in the crewel needle.

3 Cut out a second piece of silk 12 mm (½ in) larger all round than the joined piece of embroidery and silk. Turn under 12 mm (½ in) all round and tack (baste). Place wrong sides together and stitch round the edges using two strands of thread as before. Turn up about one-third of the silk to form a flap and stitch along the sides. Stitch the braid under the flap to make a strap.

SUNGLASSES CASE

This sturdy case for sunglasses is embroidered in Brighton stitch using brightly coloured tapestry wool, then lined and backed with silk.

YOU WILL NEED
Ruler
Waterproof black fine felt-tip pen
Small piece of 11-mesh single-thread canvas
Tapestry wool in the following colours: 1 skein of yellow; 3 skeins of green
Tapestry needle
Scissors
Sewing needle
Tacking (basting) thread in a contrasting colour
Small piece of green silk
Stranded cotton to match the silk fabric
Crewel needle

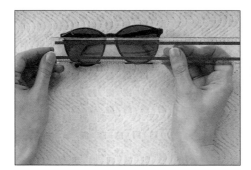

1 Measure the sunglasses to calculate how large the case needs to be. Mark out a rectangle to this size on the canvas using a black pen. To work Brighton stitch correctly, the area must divide equally into blocks of four threads.

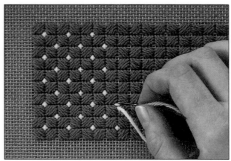

2 Cover the rectangle with Brighton stitch using green wool for the straight stitches and yellow wool for the crosses.

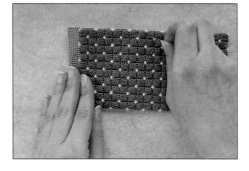

3 Cut out the embroidery leaving a border of 12 mm (½ in) all round. Turn under the raw edges and tack (baste). Cut out three pieces of green silk 12 mm (½ in) larger all round than the embroidery. Turn under 12 mm (½ in) round the edge of each piece and tack (baste).

4 Place the embroidery and one piece of fabric with wrong sides together. Stitch round the edge using two strands of matching cotton in a crewel needle. To make the back, place the remaining two pieces of green silk with wrong sides together and stitch round the edge. Place the back and front with wrong sides together and stitch round three sides.

MEMENTO BOX

Make this attractive box to keep
your tiny bits and pieces – for
example, foreign coins, paper clips or
rubber bands – and prevent them
from getting lost.

YOU WILL NEED
Turned wooden craft box with lid
Waterproof black fine felt-tip pen
Small piece of 17-mesh needlepoint
  canvas
Stranded cotton in orange, light green,
  mid green and rust
Tapestry needle
Scissors

1 Remove the
card circle from
the lid. Place it on
the canvas and draw
round it with a
black felt-tip pen.

2 Each square on
the chart
represents one
canvas intersection.
Work the design in
slanting satin stitch,
using six strands of
thread.

3 Cut out the
embroidery
slightly inside the
marked line. Mount
in the box lid
following the
manufacturer's
instructions.

HAIR CLIP

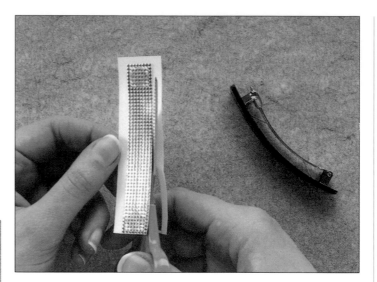

Transform a plain brown hair clip into a party piece by adding a strip of gold perforated paper embroidered with flower motifs.

YOU WILL NEED
Scissors
Small piece of gold perforated paper
Hair clip
Stranded cotton in green and pink
Tapestry needle
Fabric glue
Small paintbrush
Double-sided sticky tape

1 Cut out a strip of perforated paper large enough to cover the hair clip. Each coloured square on the chart represents one tent stitch.

2 Following the chart, work a motif at each end of the strip in tent stitch using three strands of thread.

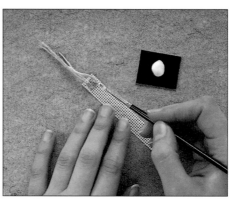

3 Secure the loose threads on the wrong side with a small dab of fabric adhesive on a paintbrush. Allow to dry thoroughly, then snip off the thread ends. Cover the back of the perforated paper with double-sided sticky tape, trimming away the surplus and taking care not to snip into the paper. Peel off the backing paper and press in position on the hair clip.

PHOTOGRAPH FRAME

Frame a favourite photograph with this needlepoint frame. The embroidery is strengthened with fabric adhesive so the surplus canvas can be cut away to leave a shaped edge.

YOU WILL NEED
Small piece of 17-mesh needlepoint canvas
Stranded cotton in beige, brown and rust
Tapestry needle
Scissors
Fabric adhesive
Craft knife
Cream card for mount to fit frame
Masking tape
12.5 cm × 18 cm (5 in × 7 in) picture frame

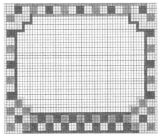

1 Work the design from the chart in tent stitch and blocks of slanting satin stitch using six strands of thread.

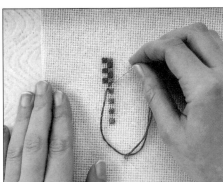

2 Using a small, sharp pair of scissors, cut away the surplus canvas carefully, close to the inner row of stitching. Seal and strengthen the wrong side of the stitches by spreading a thin layer of fabric adhesive over them.

3 Using a craft knife, cut out a rectangular window in the cream card to accommodate the embroidery in the centre. Secure the embroidery in position with strips of masking tape.

4 Centre the photograph in the aperture and secure it in position, face down, with strips of masking tape. Insert in the picture frame.

STITCHES

Cross stitch

There is more than one method of working cross stitch, but you should remember that the top diagonal stitches of each cross should always slant in the same direction, usually from bottom left to top right.

Use the first method for working individual stitches and small details on the designs, making sure you complete each cross before proceeding to the next one.

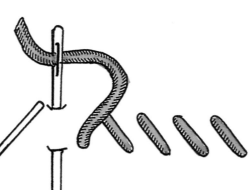

Use the second method for embroidering cross stitch over large areas as it will help you to achieve a more evenly stitched result. Begin by working a row of diagonal stitches from right to left, then complete the crosses with a second row of diagonal stitches worked in the opposite direction.

Half cross stitch

If you work just the bottom diagonal stitches, using either of the two methods shown, the stitch is then called half cross stitch.

Back stitch

Work back stitch from right to left, making small, even stitches forwards and backwards along the row, keeping the stitches of identical size.

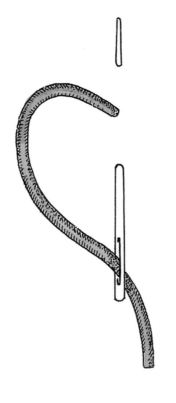

USING STRANDED COTTON

Most of the projects in this chapter are embroidered with stranded cotton. This consists of six separate strands of thread loosely twisted together. When a project requires two or three strands, first cut a length about 38 cm (15 in) long from the skein, then separate all six strands and combine them once again to give the required thickness.

CROSS STITCH CANVAS

Cross stitch fabrics come in various mesh sizes, or 'counts'. If the size specified in a pattern is not available, use the next size up or down. The design will appear slightly enlarged or condensed but the pattern will not be distorted.

CRAFT BOXES

Special craft boxes are readily available from handicrafts suppliers and haberdashery departments in large stores. These boxes come in a range of sizes and shapes and are an excellent way of displaying a special needlework design, as well as being a delightful gift. The types available include wood, brass and silver.

STARTING AND FINISHING

Do not begin with a knot at the end of your thread as this can cause an unsightly lump when your project is finished, or it may work loose and cause the stitching to unravel. Instead, secure your thread by making one or two stitches in a space which will be covered by the embroidery. When the length of thread is nearly used up, slide the needle under a group of stitches on the wrong side for about 1 cm (½ in) to anchor the thread, then cut off the loose end. You can also use this method to secure a new thread in a group of existing stitches.

USING AN EMBROIDERY HOOP

An embroidery hoop will help you to stitch more evenly and cause minimum distortion to the fabric. A hoop consists of two rings placed one inside the other with the fabric sandwiched tightly in between. The rings are secured by a screw on the outer ring.

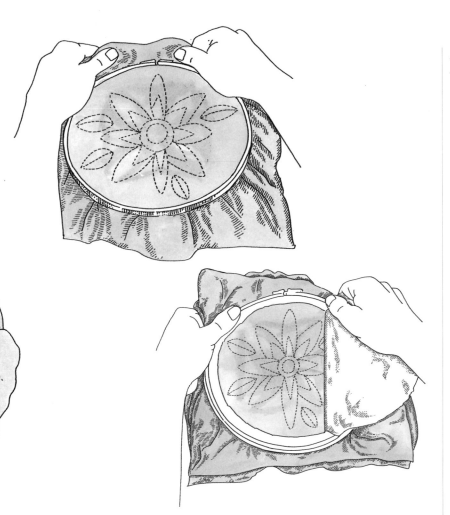

1 Spread the fabric, right side up, over the smaller hoop and press the larger hoop over the top. Tighten the screw lightly, then gently pull the fabric with your fingers until it is evenly stretched. Tighten the screw fully to hold the fabric in place.

2 On large projects, you will need to move the hoop along after one portion of the design has been completed. Protect the embroidery already worked from marks by spreading white tissue paper over the right side of the fabric before it is remounted in the hoop. Tear away the paper to expose the next area to be stitched.

WORKING FROM A CHART

Read the instructions for each design carefully before you begin to stitch. They will tell you how to mark the position of the embroidery on the fabric, and at which point on the chart you should begin stitching from. You will need to mark your starting point on the chart with a soft pencil so that the mark can be erased later.

Begin stitching from the correct point and work outwards, remembering that each coloured square on the chart represents one cross stitch to be embroidered on the fabric. The instructions will also tell you the number of woven fabric blocks you need to cover with each stitch so that the design will work out to the correct size.

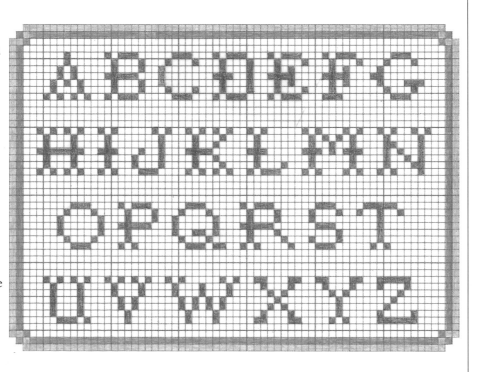

DECORATIVE TABLE MATS

A set of decorated table mats looks attractive on a polished dining table and help to protect the surface. Make matching napkins for a co-ordinated table setting.

YOU WILL NEED

For each mat: 42 cm × 30 cm (16½ in × 12 in) of 18-count ainring in ivory
Sewing needle
Tacking (basting) thread in a contrasting colour
Stranded cotton in pink, bright green and dark green (two skeins of the pink thread and two skeins of each of the green threads will be sufficient to embroider six table mats)
Tapestry needle
Pins
Sewing thread to match the fabric

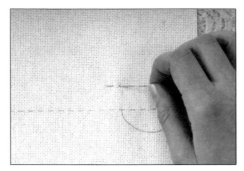

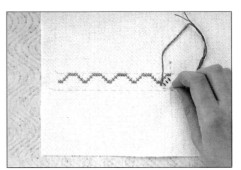

1 Mark the position of the embroidered strip about 7.5 cm (3 in) from one end of the fabric with two rows of tacking spaced 14 fabric blocks apart. Also mark the centre of the strip with a row of tacking (basting).

2 Each coloured square on the chart represents one cross stitch worked over two woven blocks in the fabric. Following the chart, embroider the design in cross stitch using three strands of thread and working outwards from the centre of the strip.

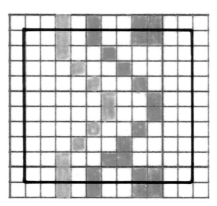

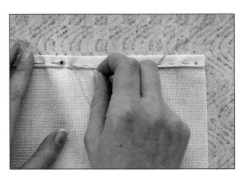

3 Taking care to fold over the corners neatly, turn a narrow double hem round the edge of the table mat, pinning and tacking (basting) in place. Secure with a row of hand or machine stitches using matching thread.

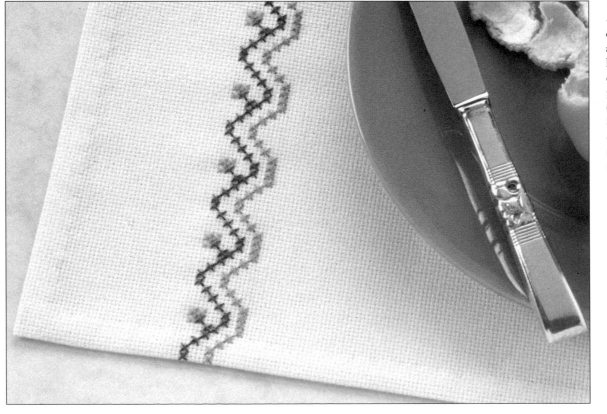

GEOMETRIC BUTTONS

This set of cross stitch buttons will liven up a plain knitted jacket or coat. To create a different effect, substitute a dark fabric for the white used here and choose pastel threads.

YOU WILL NEED
Scissors
Thin card
Six button moulds
Scraps of 14-count fine aida in
  antique white
Pins
Sharp HB pencil
Stranded cotton in red, blue and green
Tapestry needle

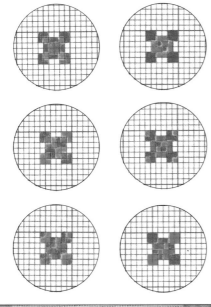

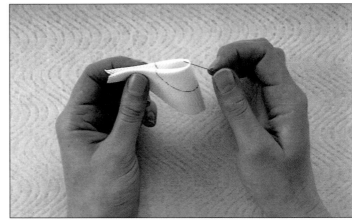

1 Cut out the correct size of circle for the chosen button moulds in thin card and use this as a template. Lay the circle on the fabric and draw round it with a sharp HB pencil. Fold the fabric in four and mark the centre with a pin.

2 Each coloured square on the chart represents one cross stitch worked over one woven block in the fabric. Following the chart, work the design in cross stitch using two strands of thread. Work out from the centre.

3 Cut out the fabric around the pencil line and stretch over the button mould following the manufacturer's instructions.

4 Attach the button backs, following the manufacturer's instructions and making sure the design will be upright on the front of each button when it is attached to the garment.

WEDDING KEEPSAKE

This charming personalized wedding keepsake is sure to delight a newly-wed couple.

YOU WILL NEED

Small piece of 11-count pearl aida in antique white
Flower thread in two shades of pink, mid blue, navy blue and green
Sewing needle
Tacking (basting) thread in a contrasting colour
Tapestry needle
Oval silver-plated frame
Sharp HB pencil
Scissors

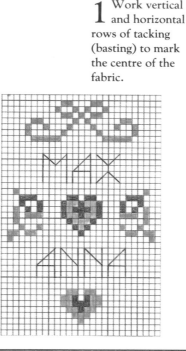

1 Work vertical and horizontal rows of tacking (basting) to mark the centre of the fabric.

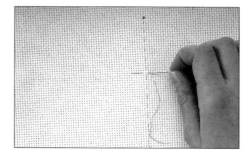

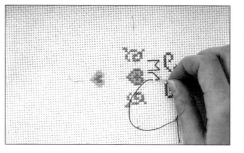

2 Each coloured square on the chart represents one cross stitch worked over one woven block in the fabric. Embroider the lettering in backstitch worked over one fabric block.

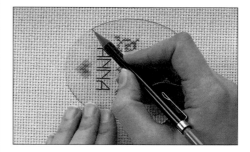

3 Remove the acetate shape from the silver frame and lay it over the finished embroidery. Draw round the acetate with a sharp HB pencil.

4 Cut out the embroidery slightly inside the pencil line. Mount in the frame following the manufacturer's instructions.

Cross Stitch

84

ALPHABET SAMPLER

Many antique samplers feature a variety of alphabets, both large and small. You may like to add your name below the lowest row of letters on this sampler using a backstitch alphabet.

YOU WILL NEED

Sewing needle
Tacking (basting) thread in a contrasting colour
Small piece of 11-count pearl aida in cream
Stranded cotton in dark pink, kingfisher blue and turquoise
Tapestry needle
Wooden cross frame
Scissors
Button thread for lacing

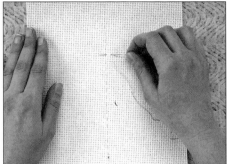

1 Work vertical and horizontal rows of tacking (basting) to mark the centre of the fabric.

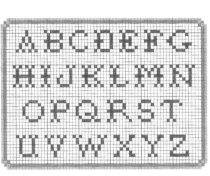

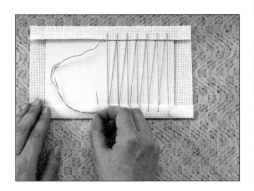

2 Each coloured square on the chart represents one cross stitch worked over one woven block in the fabric. Following the chart, embroider the design in cross stitch using three strands of cotton.

3 Remove the backing card from the frame and centre it over the wrong side of the finished embroidery. Cut away the surplus fabric leaving a border of 5 cm (2 in) all round. Fold over the fabric at the top and bottom of the card and, using button thread, make long stitches between the two fabric edges. Knot the thread at one end, tighten the stitches and secure the other end of the thread. Repeat along the other two sides. Mount in the frame.

Use this cross stitch design to embroider a set of napkins to brighten up a dinner table. The same design could also be used to decorate table mats.

YOU WILL NEED

For each napkin: 33 cm (13 in) square of 18-count ainring in ivory

Needle and tacking (basting) thread in a contrasting colour

Stranded cotton in two shades of pink, bright green and dark green (one skein of each of the pink threads and two skeins of each of the green threads will be sufficient to embroider six napkins)

Tapestry needle

Pins

Sewing thread to match the fabric

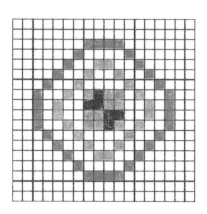

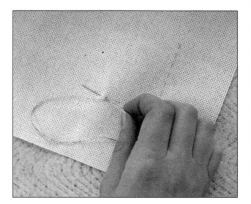

1 Mark the position of the embroidered corner motif about 5 cm (2 in) from adjacent sides of the fabric with two rows of tacking (basting).

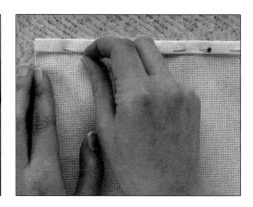

2 Each coloured square on the chart represents one cross stitch worked over two woven blocks in the fabric. Following the chart, embroider the design in cross stitch using three strands of thread.

3 Taking care to fold over the corners neatly, turn a narrow double hem round the edge of the napkin, pinning and tacking (basting) in place. Secure with a row of hand or machine stitches using matching thread.

CRYSTAL BATHROOM JAR

A hand-cut lead crystal jar with a silver-plated lid featuring an embroidered pansy motif adds a touch of luxury to any bathroom.

YOU WILL NEED
Sewing needle
Tacking (basting) thread in a
    contrasting colour
Small piece of 11-count pearl aida in
    antique white
Stranded cotton in two shades of
    yellow, fuchsia pink, wine, two
    shades of mauve, lavender, purple
    and black
Tapestry needle
Crystal craft jar with silver-plated lid
Sharp HB pencil
Scissors

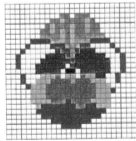

1 Work vertical and horizontal rows of tacking to mark the centre of the fabric.

2 Each coloured square on the chart represents one cross stitch worked over one woven block in the fabric. Following the chart, embroider the design in cross stitch using three strands of thread and working from the centre out.

3 Remove the acetate shape from the jar lid and lay it over the finished embroidery. Draw round the acetate with a sharp HB pencil.

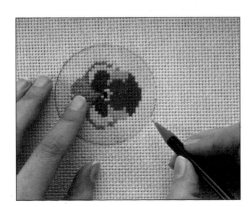

4 Cut out the embroidery slightly inside the pencil line. Mount in the jar lid following the manufacturer's instructions.

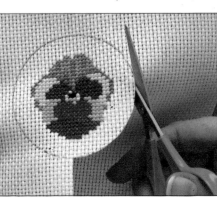

KNITTING & CROCHET TECHNIQUES

Knitting abbreviations
k = knit
p = purl
st(s) = stitch(es)
beg = beginning
inc = increase
tog = together
st st = stocking stitch
* * = instructions shown between
the asterisks must be repeated

THE BASIC STITCHES

Knit stitch
With the yarn at the back of the
work, insert the right-hand needle
through the first stitch on the left-
hand needle, wind the yarn over the
right-hand needle, pull through a
loop, then slip the original stitch off
the left-hand needle. Repeat along
the row until all the stitches have
been transferred to the right-hand
needle.

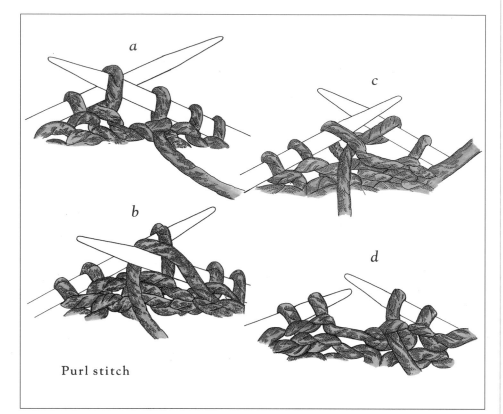

Purl stitch

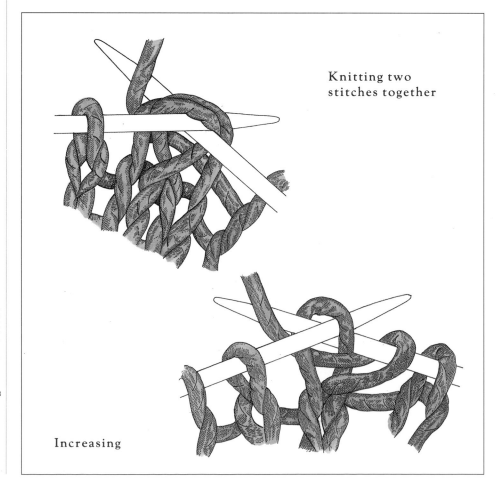

Knitting two
stitches together

Increasing

Purl stitch
With the yarn at the front of the
work, insert the right-hand needle
through the front of the first stitch
on the left-hand needle (a), wind the
yarn round the left-hand needle (b),
pull through a loop to the back (c),
then slip the stitch off the left-hand
needle (d). Repeat along the row
until all the stitches have been
transferred to the right-hand needle.

Stocking and garter stitch
To work stocking stitch, work
alternate rows of knit and purl
stitches. To work garter stitch, work
every row knit.

*Knitting two stitches
together*
Insert the right-hand needle through
two stitches on the left-hand needle
and knit them together.

Increasing
Knit or purl into the stitch in the
usual way, then knit again into the
back of the loop before slipping the
stitch off the left-hand needle.

Crochet abbreviations

ss = slip stitch
ch = chain stitch
dc = double crochet (= US single crochet)
tr = treble (= US double crochet)
dtr = double treble
rep = repeat
st(s) = stitch(es)
* = stitches shown after this sign must be repeated from this point
( ) = the stitch combination enclosed in brackets must be repeated in the order shown

THE BASIC STITCHES

Chain stitch
Wrap the yarn over the hook (a) and draw the yarn through to make a new loop (b).

a

b

Slip stitch
Insert the hook in the work, wrap the yarn over the hook, then draw the yarn through both the work and the loop on the hook in one movement.

Double treble
Wrap the yarn over the hook twice and insert the hook in the work (a), wrap the yarn over the hook and draw the yarn through the work only (b) so there are now four loops on the hook, wrap the yarn again and draw the yarn through the first two loops on the hook (c), wrap the yarn and draw the yarn through the next two loops only (d), wrap the yarn and draw through the remaining two loops on the hook (e).

a

b

c

d

e

Double crochet (US Treble crochet)
Insert the hook in the work, wrap the yarn over the hook and draw the yarn through the work only (a) so there are now two loops on the hook, wrap the yarn again and draw the yarn through both loops on the hook (b).

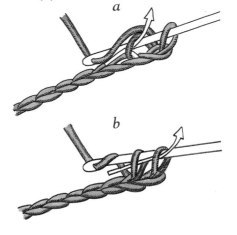

a

b

Treble crochet (US Double crochet)
Wrap the yarn over the hook and insert the hook in the work (a), wrap the yarn over the hook and draw the yarn through the work only (b) so there are now four loops on the hook, wrap the yarn again and draw the yarn through the first two loops on the hook (c), wrap the yarn and draw the yarn through the remaining two loops on the hook (d).

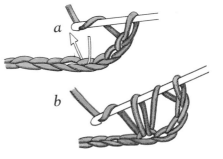

a

b

c

d

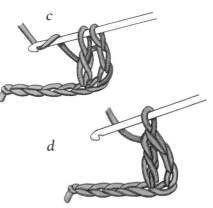

BEASTIE HAT

This hat, complete with ears, will suit any young child between the ages of 7 and 10. It is knitted in the round; if you have never done this before, this project is ideal. It is much easier than you may think and means no more sewing up or bulky seams.

YOU WILL NEED
4 double-pointed 3¼ mm (3) and 4 double-pointed 4 mm (6) knitting needles
50 g (2-ounce skein) brown double knitting (sport) yarn
Large darning needle
Scissors
Oddment of cream double knitting (sport) yarn
1 pair of 4 mm (6) knitting needles
Stuffing (batting)

TENSION (GAUGE)
Using 4 mm (6) needles, 20 sts and 24 rows to 10 cm (4 in) (st st).

HAT
Using 3¼ mm (3) needles and brown double knitting yarn, cast on 100 sts, 33 sts on each of 1st and 2nd needles and 34 sts on 3rd needle. Work 10 rounds in k 1, p 1 rib. Work should measure 5 cm (2 in).
Change to 4 mm (6) needles and k 14 rounds (st st).
Shape crown as follows:
1st round: k 8, k 2 tog 10 times round (90 sts).
2nd and every alternate round: k the round.
3rd round: k 7, k 2 tog 10 times round (80 sts).
5th round: k 6, k 2 tog 10 times round (70 sts).

Continue dec thus until 20 sts remain. K 1 round.
Next round: k 2 tog 10 times round (10 sts). Break yarn, thread through remaining sts, draw up tightly and fasten off securely. Sew in the ends.

EARS

BACK (knit 2 alike)
Using 4 mm (6) needles and brown double knitting yarn, cast on 14 sts. K 6 rows in st st. K 2 tog at beg and end of the next and following 4th row. K 1 row. K 2 sts tog at the beginning and end of the next three rows. Cast (bind) off the remaining 4 sts. Sew in the ends.

FRONT (knit 2 alike)
Using brown double knitting yarn and cream double knitting yarn, knit as for back, following chart for colour changes. Sew in the ends.

TO MAKE UP
Pin ear fronts to ear backs (with wrong sides together). Using the brown yarn, oversew the pieces together leaving the bottom edge open. Stuff and sew in place on top of the hat.

PRAM TOYS

These simple, geometric pram toys are the perfect project for a beginner or child to knit. They are also a good way to use up oddments of yarn. If they do not keep the baby happy, you could add a little seasonal embroidery and quickly turn them into unusual Christmas decorations.

YOU WILL NEED
Scraps of brightly coloured double
*   *knitting yarn*
1 pair of 4 mm (6) knitting needles
Scissors
Tape measure
Pins
Large darning needle
Stuffing (batting)
Flat plastic squeakers or small bells

TENSION (GAUGE)
This will differ according to the yarn used.

SQUARE (knit 2 alike)
Using 4 mm (6) needles, cast on 15 sts. K 18 rows in st st. Cast (bind) off. Sew in ends.

TRIANGLE (knit 2 alike)
Using 4 mm (6) needles, cast on 20 sts. K 2 rows in st st. K 2 tog at the beg and end of the next and every other row until 2 sts remain. K these 2 sts tog and pass the yarn through the last st. Sew in the ends.

DIAMOND (knit 2 alike)
Using 4 mm (6) needles, cast on 2 sts. K 2 rows in st st. Inc 1 st at the beg and end of the next and every other row until you have 14 sts. P 1 row. K 2 sts tog at the beg and end of the next and every other row until you have 2 sts. P 1 row. Cast (bind) off. Sew in the ends.

TO MAKE UP

1 Cut three 20 cm (8 in) lengths of yarn, knot together and plait (braid) to make the hanging loop. Knot the ends to fasten. Pin two matching shapes together (with wrong sides together). Place the hanging loop at the centre top with the ends between the two sides. Sew the shapes together, stitching down the hanging loop at the same time and leaving a gap of 5 cm (2 in) for stuffing (batting).

2 Stuff lightly, placing a flat plastic squeaker or bell in the centre of each toy. Sew up the gap.

CHILD'S BAG

This child's bag is made up of various different-shaped rectangles knitted in garter stitch and decorated with French knitting. It is an ideal project for a child although an adult's help will be required for the sewing up. It could easily be converted into a shoulder bag by simply knitting longer handles.

YOU WILL NEED
100 g (4-ounce skein) bright green aran-weight wool
100 g (4-ounce skein) bright orange double knitting (sport) yarn
1 pair of 5 mm (8) knitting needles
French knitting doll (knitting knobby)
Large darning needle
Scissors
Tape measure

TENSION (GAUGE)
Using 5 mm (8) needles, 14 sts and 28 rows to 10 cm (4 in) (garter stitch).

BODY OF BAG
Using 5 mm (8) needles and green aran-weight wool, cast on 28 sts. K 94 rows in garter stitch. Cast (bind) off.

BAG BASE
Using 5 mm (8) needles and green aran-weight wool, cast on 14 sts. K 24 rows in garter stitch. Cast (bind) off.

HANDLES *(knit 2 alike)*
Using 5 mm (8) needles and green aran-weight wool, cast on 6 sts. K 56 rows in garter stitch. Cast (bind) off.

LOOPS
Using a French knitting doll (knitting knobby), make 100 g (4-ounce skein) orange double knitting yarn into a length of knitted tube.

TO MAKE UP
Fold the body of the bag in half so that the knitting is sideways and sew the cast-on edge to the cast-off (bound-off) edge. Sew the base onto the body. Turn the bag right-side out so the seams are on the inside. Turn the top of the bag down 5 cm (2 in) to form a brim. Sew in place. Fold the bag in half, keeping the base square, and sew one handle onto one side of the bag on the folded top edge, leaving a 4 cm (1½ in) gap between the handle ends. Repeat on the other side. Sew in all ends.

SEWING DOWN LOOPS
Sew one end of the knitted tube to the body of the bag just under the brim. Fold over to form a loop 5 cm (2 in) long and sew the tube down 15 mm (⅝ in) away from the other end of loop. Repeat this down the length of the bag. When you reach the base, turn and come back up the length of the bag, stopping at the base of the brim. Continue zigzagging up and down the bag making loops until the whole bag is covered, spacing the rows of loops about 2.5 cm (1 in) apart.

CHRISTMAS BAUBLES

Brighten up the Christmas tree with these bright baubles. Any oddments will do and you can vary the colour schemes according to the yarns you have.

YOU WILL NEED
Oddments of 4-ply glitter yarn
3.0 mm (D) and 3.5 mm (E) crochet
   hooks
Polystyrene balls
Non-toxic gold craft paint
Small paintbrush
Tapestry needle

MEASUREMENTS
The bauble circle should measure 13 cm (5¼ in) in diameter.

BAUBLE PATTERN
Using the first colour, make 3 ch and join into a ring with a ss into first ch.
Round 1: 3 ch 15 tr into ring, join with a ss into the top of first ch.
Round 2: 3 ch 2 tr into each tr to end. Break off first colour and join in the second colour with a ss into top of first ch.
Round 3: 3 ch *2 tr into next tr, 1 tr; repeat from * around, join with a ss into first ch.
Round 4: 3 ch *tr into first tr, 2 tr; repeat from * around, join with a ss into first ch.
Round 5: 3 ch *tr into first tr 3 tr; repeat from * around, join with a ss into first ch.
Round 6: 3 ch *tr into first tr, 4 tr, repeat from * around, join with a ss into first ch. Fasten off, leaving a long piece of yarn.

HANGING LOOP
With the 3.0 mm (D) hook and the first colour, make 40 ch or a number of ch 40 cm (15½ in) long. Join with a ss into first ch. Fasten off.

TO MAKE UP
1 Paint the polystyrene balls with gold craft paint. It may be easier to paint one half of the ball and leave it to dry before continuing with the other half.

2 Thread the long piece of yarn left on the bauble circle through a tapestry needle and run a gathering stitch all the way around the outer edge of the crocheted piece.
   Place the ball in the centre of the crocheted circle. Pull on the length of yarn to gather the circle up around the ball. Fasten at the top. Attach the loop to the top of the bauble.

FABRICS, SEWING, QUILTING AND HABERDASHERY SUPPLIES

Borovicks
16 Berwick Street
London
W1V 4HP
UK
(071) 437 2180
(*Glitzy fabrics and silk*)

Chartwell Graph Paper
H W Peel & Co Ltd
Chartwell House
1C Lyon Way
Rockware Estate
Greenford
Middlesex
UB6 0BN
UK
(081) 578 6861
(*Isometric graph paper*)

Chattels
53 Chalk Farm Road
London
NW1 8AN
UK
(071) 267 0877
(*Quilts and fabrics*)

Crimple Craft
1 Freemans Way
Forest Lane
Wetherby Road
Harrogate
HG3 1RW
UK

DMC Creative World
Pullman Road
Wigston
Leicester
LE18 2DY
UK
(*Threads and cottons*)

Framecraft Miniatures Ltd
148-150 High Street
Aston
Birmingham
B6 4US
UK
(021) 359 4442
(*Craft boxes*)

Green Hill
27 Bell Street
Romsey
Hants
SO51 8GY
UK

Harlequin
Lawford
Manningtree
Essex
CO11 1UX
UK
(*Covered buttons*)

Leicester Laminating Services
71 Westfield Road
Weston Park
Leicester
LE3 6HU
UK
(*Plastic graph and template material*)

Magpie Patchworks
Department G
37 Palfrey Road
Northbourne
Bournemouth
Dorset
BH10 6DN
UK

Maple Textiles
189-190 Maple Road
Penge
London
SE20 8HT
UK
(081) 778 8049

Patchworks and Quilts
9 West Place
Wimbledon
London
SW19 4UH
UK
(*Quilts and fabrics*)

Piecemakers
13 Manor Green Road
Epsom
Surrey
KT19 8RA
UK

Pioneer Patches
Marsh Mills
Luck Lane
Huddersfield
Yorkshire
HD3 4AB
UK

Pongees Ltd
184-186 Old Street
London
EC1V 9BP
UK
(071) 253 0428
(*Silk merchants*)

Quilt Basics
2 Meades Lane
Chesham
Bucks
HP5 1ND
UK

The Quilt Room
20 West Street
Dorking
Surrey
RH4 1BL
UK

Silken Strands
33 Linksway
Gatley
Cheadle
Cheshire
SK8 4LA
UK
(*Embroidery requisites*)

The Stitchery
6 Finkle Street
Richmond
North Yorkshire
DL10 4QA
UK

Strawberry Fayre
Chagford
Devon
TQ13 8EN
UK
(*Mail order fabrics*)

Threadbear Supplies
11 Northway
Deanshanger
Milton Keynes
MK19 6NF
UK
(*Waddings/battings*)

George Weil & Sons Ltd
18 Hanson Street
London
W1P 7DB
UK
(071) 580 3763
(*Silk paints and equipment*)

George Weil & Sons Ltd
The Warehouse
Reading Arch Road
Redhill
Surrey
RH1 1HG
UK
(0737) 778868
(*Silk paints and equipment. Shop, mail order and export*)